Daily Devotions for Developing Discernment

PRODUCTIVE LEADERSHIP

I0134683

Dr. Alfonse Javed

ANM
publishers

PRODUCTIVE LEADERSHIP
Daily Devotions for Developing Discernment

ISBN: 978-0-9794929-3-8 Paperback

Published by:

ANM
publishers

Advancing Native Missions
P.O. Box 5303
Charlottesville, VA 22905
www.AdvancingNativeMissions.com

Graphic Design by:
Heather Kirk, GraphicsForSuccess.com

This book was first published in the Philippines for the Persecuted Church.

Please continue to pray for the leadership of the Persecuted Church worldwide.

"Be still, and know that I am God"
Psalm 46:10

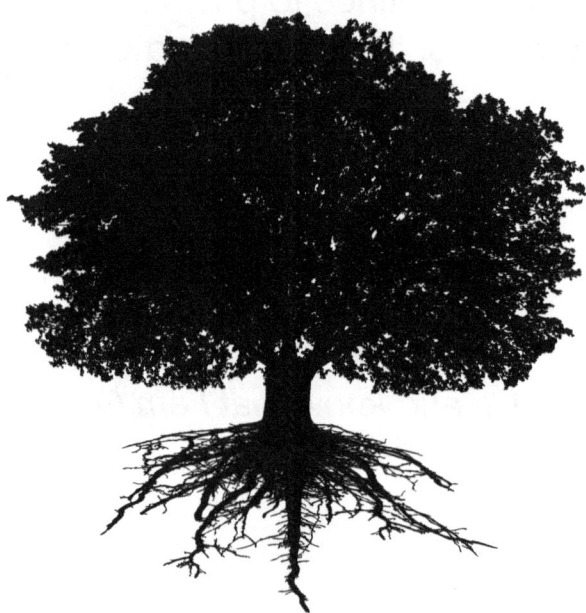

DEDICATION

I dedicate this book to the outstanding leadership of Greek Bible College, Greece, and Liberty University, USA, especially, John and Mary Gianopulos and Baldwin family.

TABLE OF CONTENTS

ACKNOWLEDGEMENTS

I want to thank many individuals for this book. Some are simply good role models of leadership, while others paved the path for me to become a better leader. First and foremost, my gratitude goes to my King and Savior Jesus Christ for leaving His throne and setting an example of the perfect leader. I thank Him for being my hope in the rough and dark times. "...Stand and see this great thing which the Lord will do before your eyes..." (1 Sam. 12:16). He alone graciously pulled me from the ditch of sin and saved my life from the enemy. "The things which are impossible with men are possible with God" (Luke 18:27). When the world closed its doors on me, He lifted me up from the depths and dried my tears. He allowed circumstances that drew me close to Himself and to shape me into a better leader. This proved His words: "Though a thousand fall at your side, though ten thousand are dying around you, these evils will not touch you" (Psalms 91:7 NLT, 2007).

I also want to thank my dear brother, Al-Tizan, from Palmer Theological Seminary of Eastern University, for recommending me for this project. I am personally indebted to a number of individuals and close friends because they offered their help in many areas. They prayed for me every day.

Dr. Alfonse Javed

PREFACE

I n August 2009, I went for an interview with a brother at the Palmer Theological Seminary of Eastern University. I did not realize the mysterious way God was working to merge relationships which would lead me to write this book. Since the time I enrolled in the doctoral degree for Organizational Leadership, I had a desire to help churches in my home country to train young men and women to be better leaders, even in the midst of persecution, poverty and lack of resources.

The lack of leadership training has always hindered the church in my country from developing an independent institution, i.e., a self-starting, self-motivated group of people, worshiping in a self-supporting way, spreading church-building and sending missionaries into neighboring towns, cities and countries. In 2006 when I was forced into exile and made the United States my temporary home (until the day God would open other doors), I began training church leaders in the states. However, my desire was to use my God given knowledge and academic experience to advance the Kingdom in those countries where the churches have no opportunity for training.

I found it almost unbelievable that churches in third world countries spend so little time in training leaders, while in the United States training is essential. Secular and religious, commercial and non-profit organizations conduct seminars and workshops for leadership training. My church back home had become a follower of cultural traditions rather than the leader willing to explore ways to preach the word of God to every corner of the world. What other churches do, my church back home follows; but who knows which churches begin with the truth and end with the truth? I like what Harold R. McAlindon said: "Do not follow where the path may lead. Go instead where there is no path and leave a trail.[1]" Following and imitating Christ should be the prime goal of every ministry; however we are living in a changing world with changing paths--who will be the leader? Sheep without a shepherd will be a delicious meal for the devourer. Christ's church cries out for good leadership in her role as model and standard for this dying world that is filled with turmoil and hopelessness.

One day I received the following email message:

> Dear Alfonse,
>
> Long time! I hope you are doing well and that 2010 is off to a good start for you. At your convenience, would you look at the email exchange below (starting from the bottom)? I'm not sure why, but your name popped up in my head, as this request to write a short book came my way. Please let me know if you sense any inkling from the Lord as you read through it.
>
> Meanwhile, God's blessings to you.
>
> Al.

One sentence gripped me and was profound to my faith: "I'm not sure why, but your name popped up in my head." I have been walking by faith since I left my country in 2003. Never for a moment did I think I would be content to live among a population of those who were merely content with what they were doing for

---

1 *Inspirational Quotes*

the Lord! I had always wanted to do more and more and more. I might even have missed the opportunity of writing this book because I was in the middle of three other book projects at the time; I also had teaching responsibilities at the New York School of the Bible.

Nevertheless, the sentence was clear, "I'm not sure why...." and my immediate understanding of the email was, "I'm sure the Holy Spirit put my name in his head." I learned long ago that when the Holy Spirit communicates to you through other brothers and sisters, you had better pay attention. After reading the original email from Doug Nichols, founder of ACTION, and forwarded by my brother, Al-Tizan, I was convinced of God's intervention in the project. Brother Doug was looking for "... some procedures, guidelines, devotionals, and encouragement in ministering the Gospel, and for compassionate care (through their limited means) to those around them-to the glory of God. There could be Bible studies, practical advice, examples and simple case studies which would encourage the poor in this way."

God was speaking to my heart through these two brothers. "What would be better—to encourage a poor church in ministering the Gospel and to reach out compassionately through their limited means? Or to train them how to be better leaders (servanthood leadership)?" I immediately began praying.

I always wanted to encourage my home church (which is one of the poorest churches in the world!) that they are commanded to minister to the poor. That, if they consider themselves poor, then they need to remember that the early church didn't have anything either. Large groups lived in basements (like shelters for homeless people), sharing food and belongings. That is the model of the Christian church.

As you can guess, when the congregation is poor, then the pastor hardly gets any financial support. As a pastor's family, my parents always felt the need to give the little they had to others because they believe in the ministry of compassion. But God was always faithful. There are so many stories of compassion, care and meeting the needs of other brethren within my family that I could write a book consisting of those stories. Let me share one story of God's faithfulness, provision and care for those who put God's will and other's needs first, those who have taken the task to minister to the poorest of poor.

I remember one winter, almost the Christmas season, when my dad had given away the last of what little money we had to a needy family. Two of my father's young disciples (one who was to become a successful pastor), came for a visit.

For most of my life, seven of us (five children and parents) lived in a one room house. This one room house was a bedroom, a kitchen, a dining room, and a TV launch site. The room was not big; two single beds, one big metal trunk and a folding bed hardly fit in it! Without any hesitation, both climbed on the beds and covered their feet with a blanket.

These two young disciples were like sons to my parents, so they were comfortable in asking for tea. "Boowa! [a very sweet term for sister] Would you mind heating up two cups of tea? It's really cold out there." We watched as my mother poured some water in a little pot and put it on a stove. It was not until another half an hour passed that one of the men asked sarcastically to my mother, "Boowa! What is taking you so long? We asked for tea [back home tea is made of water, tea leaves, a lot of milk and sugar], not for bong [a special type of food that takes the whole day to cook]." Then he turned to my father and requested humbly if he could accompany them for a walk. When they returned, they carried grocery bags filled with flour, milk, sugar and other essentials. They knew my parents should not share their needs, and it was obvious that we did not have milk or sugar to make tea. God always provided in unexpected ways.

The walk of faith my family lived, and the blessings we

received through that walk, were crucial steps in learning to depend on God. "When the needy seek water, and there is none, and their tongue faileth for thirst, I the LORD will hear them, I the God of Israel will not forsake them" (Isaiah 41:17). Jesus also promised, "Blessed are you poor, for yours is the kingdom of God" (Luke 6:20).

My personal journey with God has taken me through many trials, but God has always been faithful and delivered me from the many attacks of Satan to take my life. I learned many valuable lessons from my experiences back home, where Christians are poor, in the minority, and discriminated against. Christian history reveals that the poor and needy are often the first to respond to the call of our Lord, because they don't have the complication of possessions. When you have little, you have little concern to guard it. The smaller your earthly possessions, the greater your desire to store up heavenly treasures. When you have more (humanly speaking), you may want to hold on to it.

The rich young ruler in Scripture came to Jesus and asked, "Good Teacher, what must I do to inherit eternal life?" (Mark 10:19-22). Jesus replied: "You know the commandments: 'You must not murder. You must not commit adultery. You must not steal. You must not testify falsely. You must not cheat anyone. Honor your father and mother.'" "Teacher," the man replied, "I've obeyed all these commandments since I was young." Looking at the man, Jesus felt tender love for him. "There is still one thing you haven't done," he told him. "Go and sell all your possessions and give the money to the poor, and you will have treasure in heaven. Then come, follow me." At this the man's face fell, and he went away sad, for he had many possessions" (NLT).

Christ's love will not allow anything bad for us; because of His love we are assured of an inheritance in Heaven. Even in the midst of trials and persecution, He is faithful and continues to protect and use me-beyond my expectations! My life experiences are so similar to what my brother Doug asked for. The poor churches desperately need to rely on the sources within their communities, although it cannot compare to what the West has to offer. They have the promise of God, that He will provide, and His promises are true and worthy of testing.

Gideon lived at a time when his country was in bondage to a neighboring country. The Bible tells us that in his frustration he looked up from his work and complained, "If God is with us then why are the Midianites harming our crops and treating us badly? What happened to all those miracles that our fathers have told us about?" The angel ignored his questions saying, "Go and save Israel with the strength you have, God is sending you."

God is willing to forgive our whining and anger against Him because He wants us to be victorious in our walk with Him. It's not unusual to be frustrated when circumstances hit you hard, but it is imperative to lean on God at those times because He is going to use those situations to teach you some new and essential lessons for your faith.

When a hurting child knows that the circumstances are beyond his control, what does he do? He runs to his mother or father for help. God is our father in heaven, and in Him alone we find refuge. Thus, walking by faith takes us on a journey that no one can experience without believing that He is able to provide, protect and lead.

I am thankful that God allowed me the opportunity to write this book because many of us need a constant reminder that although we are weak, His strength is made perfect in our weakness.

I pray that this book will take you on a journey where you not only come closer to God but also to those who live around you. I pray that you may become a leader who paves the path for the next generation: that you may bring revival and an awakening in your country for the Kingdom of God.

Finally, that this book will strengthen your weak leadership areas and encourage you to become the man (or woman) God wants to use.

Dr. Alfonse Javed

INTRODUCTION

This book is a one month journey, a walk you are about to take in faith. Faith is the essence of your Christian existence. Life becomes limitless when faith takes over your walk. Earthly possessions, relationships, and even death become meaningless when faith opens your eyes to the unseen beauty and glory of our Lord Jesus who is sitting on His throne at the right hand of our Father in heaven.

We tend to think that leaving earthly possessions makes sense, but why leave relationships? Jesus said, "He who loves father or mother more than Me is not worthy of Me; and he who loves son or daughter more than Me is not worthy of Me" (Matthew 10:37, NASB). In Luke 14:26 Jesus said, "If anyone comes to Me, and does not hate his own father and mother and wife and children and brothers and sisters, yes, and even his own life, he cannot be My disciple" (NASB). When we walk by faith, then nothing or no one should cause us to stumble, not even our families. The question that Jesus was raising is this: if you had to choose between Me or a family member, who would you choose? We see the same test and illustration of faith in the life of Abraham when he was asked to sacrifice his own son.

This book is intended to encourage believers to walk in faith-without questioning or wondering whether God is there. The story of Job tells us that it cost him everything to prove that he was faithful: the result was an abundance of blessing: "The LORD blessed the latter days of Job more than his beginning..." (Job 42:12).

This book can be used as an individual devotional, a small group study, or a church activity. Each day contains a message of encouragement and a step-by-step process of learning how to be better stewards of the work to which God has entrusted us. A Christian should not take his responsibilities lightly, but rather equip himself with the best knowledge available. We should utilize 100% of our energy to more effectively serve God.

Isaiah 41:10 (NASB) could be a summary of this book. The verse says, "Do not fear, for I am with you; Do not anxiously look about you, for I am your God; I will strengthen you, surely I will help you; Surely I will uphold you with My righteous right hand."

This book offers exercises to improve one's relationship with God, family and other believers. Your one month commitment can make a huge difference in your ministry. We overlook some areas of our lives because we are always thinking, doing, or hoping that things will get better. Two main tests in this book should help you analyze your everyday activities. Whether you are productive and want to enhance your ministry or you have doubts about your productivity, the tests should allow you to see your weaker areas and how to improve them. Although the tests and exercises are designed to help you professionally, the work of the Holy Spirit remains the absolute source and solution for your productivity. Therefore, each day "walking by faith" remains the first and most significant highlight.

Your one month journey to discover what God has stored for you requires your undoubting commitment to the Word of God. You may consider a few things to be redundant, but repetition is crucial for the development process. I have included stories and illustrations to introduce you to those who have faithfully walked the walk and received the reward. The questions and comments at the end of each day are designed to challenge and encourage you. Be honest with yourself, and in a group setting, be truthful with each other; this is the only way that you will get the full benefits of this book.

My intention is that you think about what you learned in the morning, and at night do the "Nightly Activity" alone. Indeed, you can do this as a group; however, it would not reveal your personal "Overall Productivity Level" and "Spiritual Growth Level." In order to improve, enhance and develop individual leadership skills, you should do the night activity by yourself.

You may find some of the verses in the "word of encouragement" box to be out of context, but they are there to pull you out of your deep thoughts. The encouragement verses are there to remind you that God loves you, His promises are true, and regardless of our failures and weaknesses, He holds us in His hands. I pray that God may bring you to a completely new level of spiritual relationship with Him. I pray that churches and congregations may become more productive in their ministries and that the one month journey would enrich you and strengthen your compassion ministry as you trust the Lord's provision for everything. Anything and everything is possible with and for our God.

The following are the parts of each day's devotion:

1. Word of Encouragement

Word of Encouragement

"Do not let your hearts be troubled. Trust in God; trust also in me. In my Father's house are many rooms; if it were not so, I would have told you. I am going there to prepare a place for you. And if I go and prepare a place for you, I will come back and take you to be with me that you also may be where I am. You know the way to the place where I am going."
(John 14:1-4)

2. Steps toward becoming a better leader

Although prayer is the key to open the door of heaven, it is also the only way to communicate with God. But if we are praying and praying and not giving Him time to speak back to us, our prayers will not be very effective. So I encourage you to pray, but also to let the Holy Spirit speak to you in the silence.

Step 1 toward becoming a better leader is to stop praying (talking, weeping and thinking) and allow the Lord to speak to you in His unusual and usual ways.

Questions and Comments of Day 1

1. How do you think God communicates with you?

2. Are you skeptical, or open to receiving His Word through any source (even if it is not a supernatural or extraordinary

3. Questions and Comments of the Day

seek God's Will and don't look for mighty signs, because He may speak in a very usual way.

Step 2 toward becoming a better leader is to wait upon the Lord.

Questions and Comments of Day 2

1. If you are going through a test or temptation today, God is telling you He is there for you. Just have patience.

2. If you don't know what decision you should make, and both choices seem very good and potentially beneficial for ministry, sit back and wait upon Him—and listen carefully.

3. If you are waiting upon God and feeling strongly that you should give up, DON'T!! Wait as long as necessary; God will be there.

4. Nightly Activity

yourself time to hear His voice clearly.

5.   Does it seem unusual to you that God can speak to you through a very usual way?

Nightly Activity

The Nightly Activity is designed to track the productivity of your everyday life to analyze how the 31 day journey is helping you to become a better person and a better leader. It also serves as a journal. As you advance in your journey, you should look back every day and constantly check the nightly activity page to see whether you are improving. Circle a number you consider to be the overall productivity level of your day. Color the circle you consider to be your spiritual growth level today. See Appendix I.

I observed:_____

_____

I learned:_____

_____

I changed:_____

_____

Review of the day:_____

_____

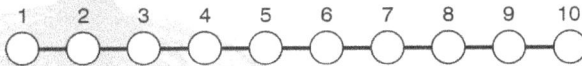

1   2   3   4   5   6   7   8   9   10

PRODUCTIVE LEADERSHIP   Daily Devotions for Developing Discernment

4

WALKING BY FAITH:
God's Unusually Usual Ways

Sometimes we tend to be oblivious of the things around us; the ways God chooses to speak to us many times pass by unnoticed because we are not paying proper attention. We chase the unknown to be sure that we are working, and probably working very hard. We try to investigate the obvious and consider the usual very unusual. When we see there is no hidden meaning and the surface is all we see, we find a deep yearning to inquire what is beneath the surface. Such instinct leads us away from our perfect God (who is not as complicated as we may sometimes think), and brings us close to our fallen nature (inherited as human). Intentionally or unintentionally we strive to be praised and rewarded for our efforts. If we simply sit back, listen carefully and let the Lord take over even though we think that we might be able to fix it, God may surprise us. I like the story of Elijah where he was waiting upon the Lord. A great and strong wind, then an earthquake, and finally a fire passed by, but God was not in them as Elijah was expecting. The Lord was in a low whisper, and the Lord asked Elijah, "What are you doing here, Elijah?" (1 Kings 19:11-13).

I wonder how many times our hasty nature urges us to give a cynical attitude towards the supernatural and leads us to believe that God speaks through us in only certain ways? Our skepticism toward God's way of communication hinders His plan to use us for His greater purpose and glory.

I wonder how many times we go unblessed because we refuse to pay attention to what is happening around us, or we get distracted easily. As Christians we need to be holding on to the Word of God. We need to do as the Psalmist writes, "I will meditate on your precepts and fix my eyes on your ways" (Ps. 119:15).

Word of Encouragement

"Do not let your hearts be troubled. Trust in God; trust also in me. In my Father's house are many rooms; if it were not so, I would have told you. I am going there to prepare a place for you. And if I go and prepare a place for you, I will come back and take you to be with me that you also may be where I am. You know the way to the place where I am going." (John 14:1-4)

As I grew up I judged the Israelites; I wondered how they could turn away from God when God had shown them miracles so clearly. I always questioned why Christ never performed a mighty miracle when He was on the cross and people were mocking Him and demanding a miracle. Today I look back at my thoughts and question myself. What if Christ had come down from the cross, would they have even then believed in Him? Realistically speaking, maybe just those who would have seen him coming down would have believed, but even among them there would have been skeptics who would have questioned the legitimacy of his crucifixion, or considered it just another of Jesus' tricks. Moses was sent to Pharaoh and performed miracles before him, yet Pharaoh considered them to be tricks and magic.

Jesus said, "He has blinded their eyes and hardened their hearts, lest they see with their eyes, and understand with their heart, and turn, and I would heal them" (John 12:40 ESV). So the problem resides in the spiritual realm of humanity, and the only way out is Christ himself. We look for mighty signs and miracles because our hearts are hardened, and our eyes are blinded to God's work in our lives and to His unusual way of interaction with us. Like Elijah, we expect His presence or voice in thunder or dazzling light when He chooses to speak to us in a very meek and ordinary way. The person of Christ as fully man and fully God does not make sense to those who don't understand how an extraordinary God can be ordinary, or how an unusual person can become so usual. Remember as you go through today that although He was not and is not ordinary, he chose to become so in order to restore your relationship with Him.

Although prayer is the key to open the door in heaven, it is also the only way to communicate with God. But if we are praying and praying and not giving Him time to speak back to us, our prayers will not be very effective. So I encourage you to pray, but also to let the Holy Spirit speak to you in the silence.

> **Step 1** *toward becoming a better leader is to stop praying (talking, weeping and thinking) and allow the Lord to speak to you in His unusual and usual ways.*

Questions and Comments of Day 1

1. How do you think God communicates with you?

2. Are you skeptical, or open to receiving His Word through any source (even if it is not a supernatural or extraordinary way of communication)?

3. Would you spend some time in prayer today and ask the Lord to open your eyes to His ways of speaking to you?

4. Have you ever had a question about God, or are you facing a problem that you have not found an answer to? I encourage you today to meditate on His Word, and to sit and relax-

because God may have already given you the answer! Give yourself time to hear His voice clearly.

5. Does it seem unusual to you that God can speak to you through a very usual way?

Nightly Activity

The Nightly Activity is designed to track the productivity of your everyday life to analyze how the 31 day journey is helping you to become a better person and a better leader. It also serves as a journal. As you advance in your journey, you should look back every day and constantly check the nightly activity page to see whether you are improving. Circle a number you consider to be the overall productivity level of your day. Color the circle you consider to be your spiritual growth level today. See Appendix I.

I observed:_____

_____

I learned:_____

_____

I changed:_____

_____

Review of the day:_____

_____

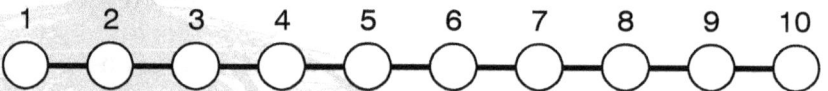

| 1 | 2 | 3 | 4 | 5 | 6 | 7 | 8 | 9 | 10 |

WALKING BY FAITH:
Seeking His Will

The Lord's Prayer is simply fascinating. This simple prayer includes almost everything to complete a Christ centered life. In the end it reads, "And lead us not into temptation, but deliver us from evil" (Matt. 6:13ESV). Every Christian falls prey to temptation; even Christ was tempted, but He defeated Satan in all of his temptations. However, there are temptations and there are tests. Temptations come sometimes as consequences of wrong choices we make that make us vulnerable to evil—and sometimes they are the direct result of our sinful nature. Tests come from God to see how faithful we are and to glorify God's name. Abraham was tested, and victoriously received promises God had never made before. David was tempted, and lost the fight against an evil and sinful nature. Whether we are being tested or tempted, seeking the will of God is the only way to go. Unfortunately, when we are being tested or tempted, our desire to seek the will of God can fade. Confusion, self-centered ambitions, and evil desires dominate our minds and hearts to devour our

> ## Word of Encouragement
>
> *"Come to me, all you who are weary and burdened, and I will give you rest. Take my yoke upon you and learn from me, for I am gentle and humble in heart, and you will find rest for your souls. For my yoke is easy and my burden is light."*
> *(Matthew 11:28-30)*

relationship with God. We do anything and everything to seek the will of God, except listening and waiting for Him.

Surrendering before Him and sitting back and letting Him take over is hard when something is truly tempting. Our flesh is constantly fighting with our spirit, and when our minds and hearts become prisoner to an impure thought, we are defenseless.

A friend of mine who has recently come to faith is going through a divorce. He is Christian and his wife is not. He tried reconciling with his wife over the matter, but she insisted on living an ungodly life. We know Jesus permitted divorce during His earthly ministry, as it is written in Matthew 5:32, "But I say to you that everyone who divorces his wife, except on the ground of sexual immorality, makes her commit adultery, and whoever marries a divorced woman commits adultery." After numerous attempts at reconciliation and sessions with a pastor, as well as professional advice from a secular counselor, he decided to give her the divorce. Now in America, it takes some time to process a divorce. Subsequently, it has been over ten months since my friend and his wife have been separated. During these ten months my friend met a beautiful Christian woman, who is totally sold for God. He found in her every single quality he could have wished for in a Christian wife. He debated whether or not he should let the woman know how he feels about her or whether he should wait until his divorce is final. So he set his heart to hear God's voice.

It gets very tempting when you want something and you know that it could be for the glory of God. It affects your capability to hear, and your circumstances take over your heart and mind, by paralyzing the spiritual being inside of you. It has been for some time that God keeps showing my friend a verse from the Bible, "But they who wait for the LORD shall renew their strength; they shall mount up with wings like eagles; they shall run and not be weary; they shall walk and not faint" (Isa. 40:31 ESV). Every time that he is down and wants to seek God's will in his life, he receives the same verse over and over again, through different resources. Sometimes it's someone in the street who hands him a flyer with the same verse, other times it's the church bulletin, a friend on the phone, or an email. It has been very encouraging for him, and for me as his friend, that he is seeking God's Will, and his ears and eyes are open to God's words. He is not seeking a big miracle or a mighty sign from God to state what God wants him to do; he knows what God wants him to do. To wait!

I have served as a pastor overseas and in the United States of America, and one thing I have noticed is that pastors and church leaders are vulnerable to more temptations than most other Christians. They are the true heroes in ministry, so just like any political or movie hero, fans want to be close to them. So if you are a leader, beware of temptations around you. Set your heart to seek God's Will and don't look for mighty signs, because He may speak in a very usual way.

> **Step 2** *toward becoming a better leader is to wait upon the Lord.*

Questions and Comments of Day 2

1. If you are going through a test or temptation today, God is telling you He is there for you. Just have patience.

2. If you don't know what decision you should make, and both choices seem very good and potentially beneficial for ministry, sit back and wait upon Him—and listen carefully.

3. If you are waiting upon God and feeling strongly that you should give up, DON'T!! Wait as long as necessary; God will be there.

Nightly Activity

The Nightly Activity is designed to track the productivity of your everyday life to analyze how the 31 day journey is helping you to become a better person and a better leader. It also serves as a journal. As you advance in your journey, you should look back every day and constantly check the nightly activity page to see whether you are improving. Circle a number you consider to be the overall productivity level of your day. Color the circle you consider to be your spiritual growth level today. See Appendix I.

I observed:_____

_____

I learned:_____

_____

I changed:_____

_____

Review of the day:_____

_____

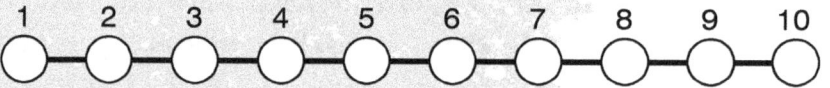

1   2   3   4   5   6   7   8   9   10

WALKING BY FAITH:
Child-Like Faith

The summer of 2007 was a very hot summer in Massachusetts. I was serving in a Christian camp near Boston, and I was at the beach when I learned the most significant and valuable lesson of my Christian walk with Christ. That particular experience has changed my perspective about God and my faith in Him. Every day we learn both physically and spiritually, and as we grow in our faith, God continues speaking to us through various ways. Sometimes it is in extraordinary ways and in other times in very ordinary ways. Nothing extraordinary happened that day, but my eyes were opened to see what I had not understood my whole life. I had never learned how to swim as a child, so the waterfront director was trying to teach me how to swim. After a week or two, he told me that my problem was that I was not trusting him. He said that I was trusting my instincts to avoid getting hurt. I was later sitting by the beach when I saw the waterfront director's wife holding her baby in her hands and floating her on the surface of water.

The baby was not crying or struggling (like I had previously done with her husband). She was doing exactly the same thing that

Word of Encouragement

"Praise be to the God and Father of our Lord Jesus Christ! In his great mercy he has given us new birth into a living hope through the resurrection of Jesus Christ from the dead." (1 Peter 1:3)

the director was trying to do with me, but my struggle and distrust didn't allow me to learn how to swim. The baby was at peace with the water, but I could not be. The baby was smiling, but I was panicking. The baby was enjoying her experience with her mom, but I was scared. It was then that the Spirit of the Lord spoke to me in an unusual usual way, of what it means to have a childlike faith.

In light of this it is very interesting to see how Jesus Christ warned those who wanted to enter in the kingdom of heaven. He said, "Truly, I say to you, whoever does not receive the kingdom of God like a child shall not enter it" (Mark 10:15). Throughout my childhood I tried to understand this, and when I became a mature Christian I was still not sure what it meant.

I knew that there is something more than just being a child in your physical body. Personally, I felt that Jesus got a little upset when the disciples were not letting the children come to him. He said, "Let the little children come to me and do not hinder them, for to such belongs the kingdom of heaven" (Matt. 19:14). Then in Matt.18:4, He elevated the state of a child to a whole new level by saying, "Whoever humbles himself like this child is the greatest in the kingdom of heaven."

I wish I could have understood why Jesus used the example of a child over and over again in reference to the heavenly Kingdom. It could have saved me years of frustrations and struggles. Today as a grown man, I observe children demonstrating basic elements of faith with unshakeable strength, and I marvel at the unraveling mystery of Jesus' words in a very simple way. These elements come down to three major traits of a true Christian life: (1) trust, (2) fear, and (3) obedience, and of course, all three in love.

Today as you go through your everyday life, try to remember: when did you last have a childlike faith? When did you last know that the Father in heaven would take care of everything? Recall the memories of your childhood, when there was a time you trusted your parents for everyday meals, clothes, and shelter. Remember when even in times of sickness they loved you and told you that you would be okay as you trusted in them. Recall the fear you had for your parents in love, and your respect for them, that made you the man or woman you are today. Recall how you were so obedient when it came to everyday chores. When mom or dad said "don't do it" or "do it," you responded obediently to them.

More than anything, a Christian person needs to become more like Christ by walking and living a childlike faith. Children trust their parents for everything because they don't know any better, and their limited life experience and span of knowledge is so little that they have to rely on their parents. A child acts according to the will of his or her parents. The trust a child has in his or her parents is needed to follow God and understand His will in our lives. The moment we attain a childlike faith we start listening to what God wants us to do, and because of our trust in Him, we willingly obey Him. Thus God's will takes over our will, and without personal effort we start relying on His intellect and power. The very desire of God's heart is that we become obedient, and through that obedience establish our relationship with Him. Jesus was so obedient to His father's will that He gave His life for us.

Step 3 toward becoming a better leader is to have faith like a child-who does not question, but trusts the decisions and plans of his parents.

Questions and Comments of Day 3

1. If you are depending on your natural instincts to run your life, then I am sorry to tell you, you are not yet ready to enter in the Kingdom of Heaven.

2. If you are running your life and feel you know how to live a life on your own power, I am sorry to tell you, you are again mistaken.

3. If you have not given up your rights and the power of being a grown person, today try to practice a childlike faith.

4. Your childlike faith is the key to becoming a better Christian and a leader.

5. Never give up, and never say you know everything—because the truth is that you don't.

6. Release your body, mind and soul into His hands and trust He will get you to the other side

Nightly Activity

The Nightly Activity is designed to track the productivity of your everyday life to analyze how the 31 day journey is helping you to become a better person and a better leader. It also serves as a journal. As you advance in your journey, you should look back every day and constantly check the nightly activity page to see whether you are improving. Circle a number you consider to be the overall productivity level of your day. Color the circle you consider to be your spiritual growth level today. See Appendix I.

I observed:_____

_____

I learned:_____

_____

I changed:_____

_____

Review of the day:_____

_____

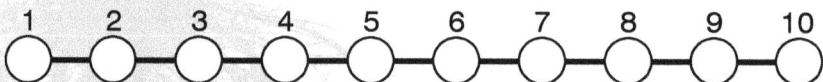

Day 4

WALKING BY FAITH:
Righteousness

When was the last time when you felt righteous? I have found myself struggling with the issue of righteousness. In the Bible, the first time the word righteous shows up is with reference to Noah's walk with God in Genesis 6:9: "These are the generations of Noah. Noah was a righteous man, blameless in his generation. Noah walked with God" (ESV). The Bible is very clear about the relationship between faith, righteousness, and walking with God.

How many times in your life you have noticed the righteous person suffering, and the unrighteous rejoicing in the riches of this world? Jeremiah cries out before God, "Righteous are you, O LORD, when I complain to you; yet I would plead my case before you. Why does the way of the wicked prosper? Why do all who are treacherous thrive?" (Jer.12:1 ESV). When you see those unrighteous people who are prospering, how do you feel? Does your heart cry out for help? My parents are in ministry: my father is a pastor and without my mother, he could never have continued the ministry. Being a pastor's family in a Muslim country is very rough and challenging. I always heard my parents repeat over and over again, "Wait a little longer, it will pass and the days of prosperity will come." Well, I don't think that in the past thirty years any of my siblings or I got rich in worldly possessions, but I learned how to be thankful to God for even minor things we had. As I walked with God, my faith in Him also grew.

During my unforgettable walks with God I always cried out to God, "Why, God, why do the righteous suffer?" There have been literally hundreds of times when death camped outside of our house and the enemy wanted to take away even the little we had, including our lives. The psalmist writes, "When the righteous cry for help, the LORD hears and delivers them out of all their troubles" (Ps 34:17). Every time God delivered my family and church from the wave of persecution, I experienced an intimate walk with our LORD. There has never been even one incident when God left us alone. The bullets were hitting, either the walls of our house, the church building, or loved ones, but we were protected by the blood of Christ; nothing could take our lives. We found comfort and peace in supernatural deliverance.

Despite God's provision and protection, there were a few times when I had doubts I felt left alone in the midst of all pain, suffering and tribulation. Many times my human nature took over my spiritual being and I lost touch with God because I decided to act on my own to remove the hurt I was going through. Many years ago I decided to walk with Christ. During this time I felt very successful (in earthly matters); I had almost everything that a man can desire. Things were somewhat less painful. I felt I was losing His touch because I was provided with a season of peace and comfort (no persecution) in my life. Deep inside of me I felt the urge to leave everything and go to Afghanistan that I might experience God's presence. This was the time when the Taliban government still had control over many parts of Afghanistan. First the weather was amazing and everything was fine. I noticed that there was peace and calm

> ## Word of Encouragement
>
> *"The LORD is a refuge for the oppressed, a stronghold in times of trouble. Those who know your name will trust in you, for you, LORD, have never forsaken those who seek you." (Psalm 9:9-10)*

in my life. I was so surprised to see that Christ was walking with me, I felt His presence.

I thanked Him and told Him that I could not be happier. As the journey continued I entered a desert I managed to get a ride with a group of people who were heading to Heart, one of the 34 provinces of Afghanistan. When they dropped me in the middle of a wasteland, I did not know what to expect next. Lo and behold, darkness prevailed and a mighty storm of disbelief and complaint such as I had never experienced before came over me. I walked for days, having eaten nothing; lack of water and food were making me physically weaker than I had ever experienced.

I started shouting at the top of my lungs, "Jesus save me! Jesus save me!" Over and over again I cried out to Him, "Where are you?" as the hot wind was bashing against my dehydrated body, and the scourging sun was unleashing its wrath on my uncovered head. When the blazing heat in this deserted area with no shelter tested me beyond my strength to endure, I shouted even louder, "Why, Jesus, why? Why have you left me?" The pain of betrayal was as clear and strong as the daylight.

I cried again, "I don't understand why I have to go through this without your peace in my heart." While I was complaining to God with all my anger and frustration, suddenly a meek and gentle voice was spoken. "Son, you wanted to experience my closeness in the midst of wilderness and pain. I was always with you. I am the one who answered your prayers and provided you with a time of rest and comfort that you intentionally abandoned." I was very ashamed of my weak faith in the Lord. I was more ashamed of my self-centered, selfish and utterly stupid step to seek my righteousness with the pretention that I was seeking God's presence. Psalm 55:22 says, "Cast your burden on the LORD, and he will sustain you; he will never permit the righteous to be moved." Our faith gets weakened by the temporary troubles in our lives, and we are prone to forget our Father in heaven who knows and provides even before we ask. Sometimes that provision comes in the form of physical comfort and a time of rest. I simply rejected the comfort because I felt uncomfortable with the comfort that was provided by God. I must confess I was displeased with the status of my righteousness. I wanted to be righteous in my own eyes, not God's. Deep down in my heart I knew I was seeking righteousness with God out of guilt, not out of love and desire to please Him. We must remember that whatever He brings into our lives out of His righteousness, whether it is good or bad in our eyes ultimately works for our good. Roman 8:28 says, "And we know that in all things God works for the good of those who love him, who have been called according to his purpose." The Apostle John writes, "If you know that he is righteous, you may be sure that everyone who practices righteousness has been born of him" (1Jn 2:29).

Step 4 toward becoming a better leader is to simply cast your burden upon Him, because He knows what you need, and at the appointed time, He will provide.

Questions and Comments of Day 4

1. If you are going through a rough time, a time of trouble and persecution, listen to what the Word of God is asking you to do.

2. Consider it joy that you have been tested for your faith, that you may learn how much God loves you.

3. Don't think that the righteous will never stand up. The day will come when you will rule with Christ.

4. Your problem, troubles and persecution are temporary. They will pass away soon. As a believer, all you need to do is simply trust in Him and His righteousness.

Nightly Activity

The Nightly Activity is designed to track the productivity of your everyday life to analyze how the 31 day journey is helping you to become a better person and a better leader. It also serves as a journal. As you advance in your journey, you should look back every day and constantly check the nightly activity page to see whether you are improving. Circle a number you consider to be the overall productivity level of your day. Color the circle you consider to be your spiritual growth level today. See Appendix I.

I observed:_____

_____

I learned:_____

_____

I changed:_____

_____

Review of the day:_____

_____

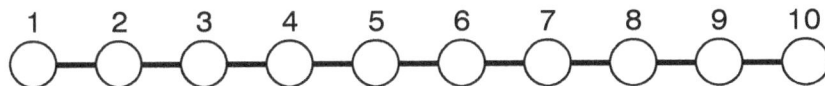

Day 5

WALKING BY FAITH:
Determination

Have you had, or are you having, one of those days when you are so discouraged? In the midst of all the discouragement, you need to remember that your determination to walk by faith will bring you close to God every day. Determination is the glue which holds vision and strategy together; so that you may fulfill the vision you have for your life, your ministry, or an organization. If you have been faithful to God and you want to be faithful to God for the rest of your life, the demon of discouragement may be trying to break your strong will to serve God and to pursue God's purpose in your life. When I face days like those, I always turn to the Bible and ask God if He could give me a tiny ray of hope and encouragement to get through the situation. Your determination to stay focused and to never give up waiting on God matters a lot for the successful completion of God's plan in your life. Let me share a true story of a man and his son, which took place right here in New York City where I live.

Word of Encouragement

"Jesus prayed, "My prayer is not that you take them out of the world but that you protect them from the evil one. They are not of the world, even as I am not of it. Sanctify them by the truth; your word is truth. As you sent me into the world, I have sent them into the world."
(John 17:15-18)

In 1883, a creative engineer named John Roebling was inspired by an idea to build a spectacular bridge connecting New York with Long Island. However, bridge building experts throughout the world thought that this was an impossible feat and told Roebling to forget the idea. It just could not be done. It was not practical. It had never been done before.

Roebling could not ignore the vision he had in his mind of this bridge. He thought about it all the time and he knew deep in his heart that it could be done. He just had to share the dream with someone else. After much discussion and persuasion, he managed to convince his son Washington, an up-and-coming engineer, that the bridge could be built. Working together for the first time, the father and son developed a plan for how it could be accomplished, and how the obstacles could be overcome. With great excitement and inspiration, and the headiness of a wild challenge before them, they hired their crew and began to build their dream bridge.

The project started well, but when it was only a few months underway, a tragic accident on the site took the life of John Roebling. Washington was injured and was left with a certain amount of brain damage, which resulted in him not being able to walk, or talk, or even move. Everyone had a negative comment to make, and felt that the project should be scrapped since the Roeblings were the only ones who knew how the bridge could be built. In spite of his handicap, Washington's mind was as sharp as ever. He was never discouraged; he still had a burning desire to complete the bridge. He tried to pass on his enthusiasm and inspire some of his friends, but they were too daunted by the task. As he lay on the bed in his hospital room with the sunlight streaming through the windows, a gentle breeze blew the flimsy white curtains apart and for just a moment, he was able to see the sky and the tops of the trees outside. It seemed that there was a message for him not to give up. Suddenly an idea hit him. All he could do was move one finger, but he decided to make the best use of it. By moving this finger, he slowly developed a communication code with his wife. He touched his wife's arm with the finger, indicating to her that he wanted her to call the engineers again. Then he used the same method of tapping her arm to tell the engineers what to do. It seemed foolish, but the project was under way again.

For 13 years Washington tapped out his instructions with his finger on his wife's arm, until the bridge was finally completed. Today the spectacular Brooklyn Bridge[2] stands in all its glory, as a tribute to the triumph of one man's indomitable spirit, and his determination not to be defeated by circumstances. It is also a tribute to the engineers and their team work, and to their faith in a man who was considered mad by half the world. It also stands as a tangible monument to the love and devotion of his wife, who for 13 long years patiently decoded her husband's messages and told the engineers what to do.

Paul gives an example of how a Christian should be determined. "Do you not know that in a race all the runners run, but only one receives the prize? So run that you may obtain it. Every athlete exercises self-control in all things. They do it to receive a perishable wreath, but we an imperishable. So I do not run aimlessly; I do not box as one beating the air. But I discipline my body and keep it under control, lest after preaching to others I myself should be disqualified" (1 Corinthians 9:24-27 ESV).

Step 5 toward becoming a better leader is to remember that your determination is the glue to hold your vision and strategy together.

Questions and Comments of Day 5

1. If Roebling did not give up even with his extreme physical disabilities, why should you?

---

2 See the image of the Brooklyn Bridge in the Appendix VII

2. Roebling's dream was to build something which would last for a certain time, but you are building the Kingdom of God, which is for eternity.

3. Your determination is imperative to the successful execution of God's purpose in your life and in your ministry.

Nightly Activity

The Nightly Activity is designed to track the productivity of your everyday life to analyze how the 31 day journey is helping you to become a better person and a better leader. It also serves as a journal. As you advance in your journey, you should look back every day and constantly check the nightly activity page to see whether you are improving. Circle a number you consider to be the overall productivity level of your day. Color the circle you consider to be your spiritual growth level today. See Appendix I.

I observed:_____

_____

I learned:_____

_____

I changed:_____

_____

Review of the day:_____

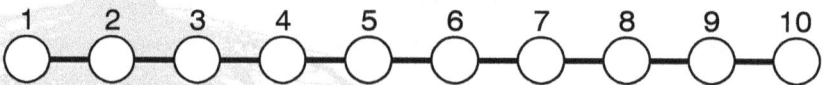

_____

1   2   3   4   5   6   7   8   9   10
○—○—○—○—○—○—○—○—○—○

WALKING BY FAITH:
Generosity

It was a bright, sunny day in the Broadway Street of Manhattan, New York City, and I was on my way to my ministry, when an unusual sign got my attention. The sign read, "I am hungry." Immediately I saw the need of food and a drink, but when I got near to the person, I noticed that he was in very fit physical condition. He could have worked to make some money to feed and clothe himself. I did not judge him for doing what he was doing, but I saw that it presented an opportunity to plant a seed in his life. Like a Good Samaritan, I met his need first, because he wanted food. So I asked him what he would like to eat. He replied, "hot soup." It took me about a half an hour to find soup, and when I got back, he was there. I got to talk to him and share about Christ's compassion, and it was at this point that he refused to continue the conversation. I thought there are many people who can see his physical hunger and need, but there are a few who would be able to spot his spiritual need. Jesus answered Satan, "It is written, 'Man shall not live by bread alone, but by every word that comes from the mouth of God'" (Matt 4:4 ESV).

People from all over the world come to America and desire to see New York City. The city has been the trademark of worldly riches and glamour. People move to NYC from both overseas and within the United States to fulfill their dreams. Nevertheless, this is the city where I have found the worst poverty. God brought me here to teach me about the Kingdom of Heaven vs. the kingdom of earth. I never gave enough to the poor and needy, until I moved here. In the past six months I have experienced generosity and compassion toward others. The little I have I share with others, though many times I hardly have money to travel from point A to point B. I have felt moved by the Holy Spirit to share my earthly possessions with those who have come to New York City to find their dream lives, and have now lost everything—or those who are simply ashamed to go back to their home towns because people will be very disappointed in them.

I have never been rich in earthly possessions, and as a missionary one has to rely on financial gifts received from other Christians. So buying a meal for someone means fasting for that meal yourself. Sometimes, when I was thirsty and wanted to buy a drink, I didn't, because I wanted to save money for a meal. But, if I then saw someone in need, the money went to him or her, leaving me thirsty and hungry. Now here is the important thing. If I had no money, I wouldn't have felt guilty and obligated to help others. But if I do have money, even though it is only enough to buy one meal for myself, and I come across someone who is poorer than I, then the money will be spent to bring physical comfort in the needy person's life.

If you are sharing or giving to someone because you have in abundance, that does not prove your generosity. But, to give when you don't have is true generosity. Jesus saw the old lady in the Temple and considered her offering

Word of Encouragement

"Knowing that you were not redeemed with perishable things like silver or gold from your futile way of life inherited from your forefathers but with precious blood, as of a lamb unblemished and spotless, the blood of Christ."
(1 Peter 1:18-19)

to be more than that of anyone else, because she gave all she had, which was only a penny. Paul encourages Christians, "for in a severe test of affliction, their abundance of joy and their extreme poverty have overflowed in a wealth of generosity on their part" (2 Cor. 8:2). Giving to God and meeting the needs of the poor brings you close to God and away from worldly possessions. Jesus said, "but lay up for yourselves treasures in heaven, where neither moth nor rust destroys and where thieves do not break in and steal" (Matt. 6:20).

A good leader does not use his power or worldly possessions to intimidate others; neither does he brag about it, nor does he consider it his. When I started out as a full time missionary, financially I went from 100 to 0. I had to raise my support, but I had never asked others for money before. I would never forget what a friend of mine told me. He said, "Christians need to know that whatever they have is God's, including their money. They are supposed to be sharing it with other Christians. So when you ask, you are not asking for yourself. It is for God, the one to whom your possessions belong in the first place."

When I look at good leaders, most of them have one thing in common; they were not hungry for power or worldly possessions. If you are a leader who has the position because you like to be in charge, or to sit in a special seat, then my friend, you are far away from servanthood leadership. The model of Christ shows generosity toward all humanity. He was so generous that He left His throne in heaven and came to this filthy world and became like us to reach out to the lost. The writer of the book of Hebrews states, "…putting everything in subjection under his feet. Now in putting everything in subjection to him, he left nothing outside his control. At present, we do not yet see everything in subjection to him. But we see Him who, for a little while, was made lower than the angels, namely Jesus, crowned with glory and honor because of the suffering of death, so that by the grace of God he might taste death for everyone" (Heb 2:8-9 ESV).

If we remember that everything belongs to God, then we would not worry about worldly possessions, except to do good with what has been entrusted to us. The Gospel of Luke gives a warning for those who would consider their leadership as a way of exercising power, "He [God] has brought down the mighty from their thrones and exalted those of humble estate" (Luke 1:52 ESV).

Step 6 toward becoming a better leader is leaving worldly possessions behind and being generous in everything you have: in love, kindness, grace, compassion and care.

Questions and Comments of Day 6

1. Today, if you see a needy person, meet his or her need.

2. Try to learn through generosity how to reach out to others for Christ.

3. If you trust in the Lord and share, even the little you have with others, you will experience how joy can take over your spirit.

4. Walking in faith is not possible when you are trying to hold worldly possessions in one hand and faith in the other.

5. You will deliberately decide not to practice power when you could, rather, be graceful and merciful, as your Father in heaven makes you a better leader and person.

Nightly Activity

The Nightly Activity is designed to track the productivity of your everyday life to analyze how the 31 day journey is helping you to become a better person and a better leader. It also serves as a journal. As you advance in your journey, you should look back every day and constantly check the nightly activity page to see whether you are improving. Circle a number you consider to be the overall productivity level of your day. Color the circle you consider to be your spiritual growth level today. See Appendix I.

I observed:_____

_____

I learned:_____

_____

I changed:_____

_____

Review of the day:_____

_____

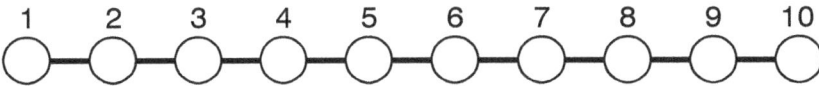

Day 7
WALKING BY FAITH:
Optimism

L ast night I was with a group of young men and women who have registered for the Leadership Development Program. The way I have designed the program should encourage an ordinary person to become an extra-ordinary person. Sometimes it is just a little longer process than many want to wait to achieve. We know there are some who are natural leaders. I mean, God has blessed them to be leaders. Then there are those who need to be taught how to be leaders. There is no principle that says that an ordinary person can't be a leader. Every person is a leader to some extent. Whether the person is a negative leader or a positive one is a different story. History has seen both types of leaders, and I am very certain you are aware of such leaders. I assure you, Christian ministries are not immune to negative leadership. In our ministries, we see those who are able to lead small or large groups; they have the ability to influence their followers positively and negatively.

The group of young men and women with whom I was working was very optimistic in the first week, which made me think that the rest of the four weeks were going to be very productive. Unfortunately, as the second week approached, the optimistic behavior and energy started disappearing. The expectations they had before they arrived on campus were found to be, on some level, unrealistic. They were expecting some magic talk or pill to transform them into leaders, or better leaders. But the curriculum I had designed was a step by step approach. The first week they were supposed to get to know each other and to get familiar with the program. Also, I wanted to see and observe their spiritual and physical gifts/talents. The level of optimism about your leadership style, family, ministry and work place determines how well you would do as a whole team. So my task was to construct the quality of optimistic leadership among them. Many times as Christians we ask God for one thing and He gives another, which frustrates us. God's way of looking at the problem is very different from ours. We tend to look at

Word of Encouragement

"According to my earnest expectation and hope, that I shall not be put to shame in anything, but that with all boldness, Christ shall even now, as always, be exalted in my body, whether by life or by death. For to me, to live is Christ, and to die is gain."
(Philippians 1:20-21)

the surface and try to fix it; we do not want to investigate what caused it. Because of our ignorance we receive temporary fixing, but in the long run we face worse misery.

If the wound is deep, simply putting a bandage on it is not going to heal it. It needs proper care and cleansing. When we ask God for something, we need to trust that He is fixing our deeper problem first so that we will not suffer over and over again. A permanent solution takes time compared to a temporary solution. A permanent solution costs more, too.

Therefore, if you are not optimistic about the end results of the everyday process of healing in your life, most likely you will give up soon after God starts working in your life. Make sure you are not looking for a temporary fix, but a permanent solution; a permanent solution will come with a positive attitude. Walking by faith gives you another perspective on life. You stop sniffing around to discover options to resolve your issues, because you know that there is only one perfect solution and God alone knows it, and through faith you can attain it. It might come late, but when it comes it will be the best and perfect solution. Your optimism is imperative for your walk with God. The following poem (by an unknown poet) is a good example of God's way of fixing the deeper issues and answering our prayer to make us better people and leaders:

> *I asked for Strength… And God gave me*
> *Difficulties to make me strong.*
>
> *I asked for Wisdom… And God gave me*
> *Problems to solve.*
>
> *I asked for Prosperity… And God gave me a*
> *Brain and Brawn to work.*
>
> *I asked for Courage… And God gave me*
> *Danger to overcome.*
>
> *I asked for Love… And God gave me*
> *Troubled people to help.*
>
> *I asked for Favors… And God gave me*
> *Opportunities.*
>
> *I received nothing I wanted… I received*
> *everything I needed!*

Jesus said, "You are wrong, because you know neither the Scriptures nor the power of God" (Matt. 22:29 ESV). The Scriptures tell us that God loves us and that His love compels Him to help us. As a father, He wants us to learn through circumstances how to be a better person.

> ***Step** 7 toward becoming a better leader is to be optimistic and do not let the temporary solution waste your time and ruin your positive attitude.*

Questions and Comments of Day 7

1. Today I encourage you to take another step (a gigantic one); be optimistic about any problem or issue you are going through. Trust that God is at work in your life and in the situation you are facing.

2. Have you ever preferred a temporary solution to get through the day or the moment? It shows human hastiness to attain what we need (or want), even if it is to be available only for a moment.

3. God sees the full picture, and He knows that the temporary solution will not help and could not be the right choice for you, so He decides the right solution for you. Remember you have asked him to help you, so trust Him and He will fix it forever.

4. If you are going through broken relationships, family or church problems, financial problems, job troubles, or even if you are sick, ask God the Father in the name of Jesus-and wait upon Him. He will start His work in your life right away. You might see the result in a while, but the reason it might take longer is because God doesn't do temporary work. He is perfect and does everything with perfection.

5. If you are an optimistic person and for some reason you feel a little down-don't worry. Remember you are just a human being, and it is okay to be down sometimes. Dig into the word of God and restore your optimism. Personally, I like the psalms for such encouragement.

Nightly Activity

The Nightly Activity is designed to track the productivity of your everyday life to analyze how the 31 day journey is helping you to become a better person and a better leader. It also serves as a journal. As you advance in your journey, you should look back every day and constantly check the nightly activity page to see whether you are improving. Circle a number you consider to be the overall productivity level of your day. Color the circle you consider to be your spiritual growth level today. See Appendix I.

I observed:_____

_____

I learned:_____

_____

I changed:_____

_____

Review of the day:_____

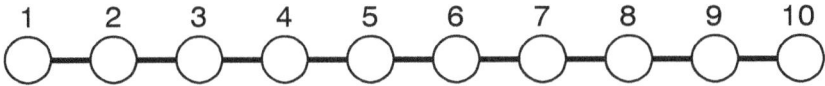

_____

| 1 | 2 | 3 | 4 | 5 | 6 | 7 | 8 | 9 | 10 |

Day 8

WALKING BY FAITH:
Do Good!

Proverbs 3:27 says, "Do not withhold good from those to whom it is due, when it is in your power to do it." What does this mean? Is there a time when doing good is not in your power any longer? Christ did good even on the cross when He forgave those who persecuted Him. Perhaps we withhold good because we see others not acting in a right manner. Or it might be because we were ignorant of the rewards of good acts. Humans are naturally inclined to seek rewards for things, either spiritual or physical rewards. We tend to do good in order to receive a reward. David writes, "Turn away from evil and do good; seek peace and pursue it" (Psa. 34:14 ESV). David was a man after God's heart, and a warrior and a just king. He made Israel a victorious and unprecedented nation during his reign. Of course, the hand of the Sovereign God was upon him, but he was obedient to His command. Even when he committed sin before God's eyes, he begged for mercy. 2 Sam 24:10 says, "But David's heart struck him after he had numbered the people. And David said to the LORD, 'I have sinned greatly in what I have done. But now, O LORD, please take away the iniquity of your servant, for I have done very foolishly.'" When you intend to do good, and yet foolishly you do evil, remember God is a forgiving God.

David's leadership style was based on doing good, even when Saul was trying to kill him. Many times God delivered King Saul into David's hand, yet David chose to do good. Walking by faith makes you understand the incomprehensible. Jesus' command, "And if you do good to those who do good to you, what benefit is that to you? For even sinners do the same" (Luke 6:33 ESV), sounds very unfair and unreasonable to those who don't walk by faith. But to those who have crucified their lives with Christ and no longer live by the ways of the flesh but by the Spirit, they are given the understanding of doing good to your enemy. Jesus became the supreme leader by commanding, "But love your enemies, and do good, and lend, expecting nothing in return, and your reward will be great, and you will be sons of the Most High, for He is kind to the ungrateful and the evil" (Luke 6:35). Jesus knew how hard it is to love your enemy because He practiced it Himself; yet He commanded such because it is the greatest good a human can do.

I have been personally persecuted for my faith; my whole family suffered because of their faith, but one day I received news. The gang leader, who had been involved in 90% of the attacks on our house and church, got sick. My parents went to his house when no one came to his help. They offered food, money, medication and care. The man could not survive. He died,

Word of Encouragement

"Do not complain, brethren, against one another, that you yourselves may not be judged; behold, the Judge is standing right at the door... Behold we count those blessed who endured."
(James 5:9,11a)

and my dad conducted his funeral. Then another man who was on his death bed called for my father. My father and mother knew that he had been part of the opposition party. Previously, my father, two brothers, and I myself had been accused of a murder attempt in a well-planned plot against our family to stop the work of the Lord. So caution was in our best interests.

This plot had been a false accusation where a man (covered in scars) appeared in the court and lied that we had tried to kill him.

He had deep wounds. The allegation was filed in the judiciary process, witnesses were called, and the complaint was read. My name was mentioned as one of the perpetrators who was holding the victim from the back. The judge asked for me, and my dad responded that I had "been living abroad for a year when the incident happened." Now all the truth was out, because of one tiny mistake the enemy made! The Judge ordered the release of my family-with a caution to the opponents that they may not bring more false accusations against my family and church. Since then, my family was wary about the next plot. The enemy may have perfected a plan, based on the previous failure, to trap us and destroy the ministry. After prayers, my dad and mom decided to go and visit this leader of the opposition party. When they entered his room, the man in the bed requested prayer, and asked his family to leave the room. It was very dangerous, but my parents were walking by faith. Now my dad, mom, and the man were alone in this tiny room. The man started crying and said the reason he had asked for them was because he wanted to confess something before he died. He confessed that he was hired to murder my father, but in a few attempts, somehow (miraculously) my father was not hurt. This led the man to believe that the true God is with my dad and his ministry.

When you do good and love your enemy because God wants you to, then the reward is greater in heaven. A story is told about a king who had a boulder placed on a roadway. Then he hid himself and watched to see if anyone would remove the huge rock. Some of the king's wealthiest merchants and courtiers came by and simply walked around it. Many loudly blamed the king for not keeping the roads clear, but none did anything about getting the big stone out of the way. Then a peasant came along carrying a load of vegetables. On approaching the boulder, the peasant laid down his burden and tried to move the stone to the side of the road. After much pushing and straining, he finally succeeded. As the peasant picked up his load of vegetables, he noticed a purse lying in the road where the boulder had been. The purse contained many gold coins and a note from the king indicating that the gold was for the person who removed the boulder from the roadway. The peasant learned what many others never understand.

When you do good without expecting a reward, you will find a deeper joy and satisfaction than you may have experienced ever before. The King of kings in heaven who sees you-even when no one else sees you or notices will reward you out of His good will.

Step 8 toward becoming a better leader is to let your old being go, wear your renewed being, and do good! Even when you do not want to.

Questions and Comments of Day 8

1. Today try to do good without looking for a reward; do unconditional good.

2. Have you ever looked back at your life and tried to see who wronged you, and to whom you did wrong? If you have not done that before-do it now. It will set you free from anger and frustration. Let the past go away, and starting from today, experience a blessed walk with God by doing good to others even if they are your enemies.

3. Do you consider someone an enemy, or is there someone in your life you do not want to see, speak to, or even think about who makes you too angry? The Scriptures encourage you to do good to that person. Today, take another step in your walk with God by doing good. God did the same for us. We deserve His wrath because of the animosity between God and us. God initiated our redemption in His goodness by sending His only Son Jesus to pay the price of sin. By giving His life for us, He showed His perfect and ultimate goodness to mankind.

Nightly Activity

The Nightly Activity is designed to track the productivity of your everyday life to analyze how the 31 day journey is helping you to become a better person and a better leader. It also serves as a journal. As you advance in your journey, you should look back every day and constantly check the nightly activity page to see whether you are improving. Circle a number you consider to be the overall productivity level of your day. Color the circle you consider to be your spiritual growth level today. See Appendix I.

I observed:_____

_____

I learned:_____

_____

I changed:_____

_____

Review of the day:_____

_____

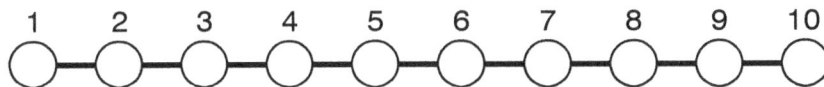

WALKING BY FAITH:
Living by Faith

Heb.11:1 says, "What is faith? It is the confident assurance that what we hope for is going to happen; it is the evidence of things we cannot yet see."

The very first message I ever delivered was on faith. I remember very vividly, that I was only 15 years old. My dad (who is a pastor) was in bed, due to a leg broken during an accident on his way to daily visitation. (Our family lived daily on what was given by the Christian people as donations, so every evening my mom and dad had to go; otherwise there would be no meal on the table). So my older brother and I started taking turns to go out with my mother for daily visitation. It came as a surprising request when my mother declared in a very sweet voice, "I want you to share something with the family we are about to visit tonight!" It wasn't the end of the sentence; she continued with a deep voice, "... I don't know how long it will take your dad to get back on his feet." I was already convinced-also, when your mom says something, you better do it! I prayed and asked God to help me. We got to the house and, after prayer; I opened the book of Hebrews and started with Heb.11:1. I believe the reason I felt the urge to start with this particular verse was because it is the Scriptural definition of faith. Four words stood out to me:

- Confidence
- Assurance

- Hope
- Evidence

We will look at each word in a little detail as the time passes.

Faith has been the primary focus of my life and my sermons, lectures, and writings. Although I was young physically and spiritually at that point of my life, yet I understood the basics of faith. However, I would be learning the deep meanings of faith in following years. Faith was about to become the ingredient of my basic philosophy about life and death. There are many things we as human beings think we can do on our own, but walking and living by faith means you can't do anything without God. Also many times our trust in God's plan seems a little weaker when we try to help God. Who are we to help the Almighty? I have heard many preachers and speakers say, "God needs our help to complete His mission in this world." Does God really need our help? If that is the case, then I am sorry to disappoint you. You are not worshiping the right God. Our God is able to do whatever He wants, whenever He wants, and the way He wants. He has hidden wisdom when He delays His plans. Our job is to simply walk and live by faith, and let the healer heal, and the provider provide. He has wisdom behind His creation. Our faith may play a crucial role in allowing His plan to be successfully executed in our lives and in the lives of others, but certainly it is He alone who accomplishes everything by His own power. Also, our lack of faith in Him and His timing certainly plays a crucial role in our lives and others.

A man once found a butterfly cocoon. One day a small opening appeared. He sat and watched the butterfly for several hours, as it struggled to force its body through that little hole. Then it seemed to stop making any progress. It appeared as if it had gotten as far as it could, and it could go no further. So the man decided to help the butterfly. He took a pair of scissors and snipped off the remaining bit of the cocoon. The butterfly then emerged easily.

But it had a swollen body and small, shriveled wings. The man continued to watch the butterfly because he expected that, at any moment, the wings would enlarge and expand to be able to support the body, which would contract in time.

Neither happened! In fact, the butterfly spent the rest of its life crawling around with a swollen body and shriveled wings. It never was able to fly. What the man, in his kindness and haste, did not understand was that the restricting cocoon and the struggle required for the butterfly to get through the tiny opening, were God's way of forcing fluid from the body of the butterfly into its wings, so that it would be ready for flight once it achieved its freedom from the cocoon.

Word of Encouragement

"Let us therefore draw near with confidence to the throne of grace, that we may receive mercy and may find grace to help in time of need."
(Hebrews 4:16)

There are times when we want to do good, but our lack of faith in God hinders or paralyzes His plan in our lives and in the lives of others. Jesus said to the blind man, "According to your faith be it done to you" (Matt.9:29 ESV). God allows things to happen according to our faith. Jesus responded to his disciples when they were astonished about the fig tree, "Truly, I say to you, if you have faith and do not doubt, you will not only do what has been done to the fig tree, but even if you say to this mountain,'Be taken up and thrown into the sea,' it will happen" (Matt.21:21 ESV).

According to Hebrews 11:1, the definition of faith contains four big words. The first one is "confident," or "confidence." As I grew physically and spiritually, I became more confident of those things I do not see and would not understand, even if I could see. I have been teaching for over a decade, and in my recent teaching I have started mentioning that the spiritual world is more real than the physical world. In your life you come to a point where you realize the truthfulness and the reality of our existence, and the moment you acknowledge the presence of a Supreme Being in this world (the All-Knowing Sovereign who surrounds us) you open yourself up to a whole new realm. I am not talking about the possibilities of spiritual being. I am talking about the presence of the spiritual beings around us all the time, even at the very moment you are reading this. I teach at the New York School of the Bible in New York City, USA. I was teaching a course on theology; in systematic theology, the lecture was on angelology and demonology. The topic brought goose bumps to some of the students. This topic is well discussed in the Eastern world, but lack of understanding in the West has made it almost factitious. Anyhow, the world of demons is the evidence of Satanocracy in this world. Matthew 4:9 says, "Again, the devil took him [Jesus] to a very high mountain and showed him all the kingdoms of the world and their splendor and he said to him, 'All these I will give you, if you will fall down and worship me.'" The real world is the evidence of Satan's kingdom, but the spiritual world is the reality of the heavenly kingdom. The world we live in is just a shadow which will pass, but the world we are confident to live in under the rule of God is real and perfect.

The writer of Hebrews reminds the church, "Don't, therefore, abandon that confidence of yours, it being a great reward. For you need endurance, so that when you have done the will of God you may receive what was promised" (Heb.10:35 ESV). In our restless and struggling lives things are not promised to get better when we become Christians; but it is through confidence in the One Who is in us, that He is greater than the one (Satan) who is in the world. Such confidence is the foundation of our Christian life; through Him we can do anything. Our surrender before God makes us victorious and fearless, and our confession before Him releases us from the bondage of worry and weakness, especially when we confess before Him that we are weak and worried. He knows it already, but our confession becomes an invitation for Him to come and intervene. It does not mean that we will not face trials and will not go through everyday challenges; certainly we can't avoid the effects of sin in this world. The encouragement for Christians is this; that troubles of the world may pile up around us and over us, but we will get through them. Nevertheless, we have confidence in the victory of Christ. He said, "do not be afraid; I am the first and the last, and the living one. I was dead, and see, I am alive forever and ever; and I have the keys of Death and of Hades" (Rev.1:17b-18). This makes us fearless, and worry free. In Luke 12:22 Jesus said, "Therefore, I tell you, do not worry about your life what you will eat, or about your body, what you will wear," and the same chapter (verse 32) says, "do not be afraid, little flock, for it is your Father's good pleasure to give you the kingdom." Jesus said, "Blessed are the poor in spirit, for theirs is the Kingdom of heaven" (Matt.5:3). I know very well that in our natural being it is difficult for us to be confident of all the promises we have in Him; because our natural selves encourage us to lose our confidence in the unseen world, in the heavenly Kingdom, in the glorious reign of our King Jesus, and in the unfathomed joy we will celebrate in eternity. We have confidence that, "Heaven and earth will pass away, but my [Jesus'] words will not pass away." As Jesus taught His followers, "Be on guard so that your hearts are not weighed down with dissipation and drunkenness and the worries of this life, and that day does not catch you unexpectedly" (Luke 21:34).

Step 9 toward becoming a better leader is to live by faith. Walking by faith and living by faith proves you are a leader of integrity. Believing is walking by faith, and when you do what you believe you are living by faith. The application of your walk is the living experience of faith. Also, be confident of yourself that you are in God's hand and God will use you. Be confident that all the power has been given to Christ and He has extended that power to us on His behalf.

Questions and Comments of Day 9

1. Do you live by faith? In other words, do you wait upon God to provide everything in His time?

2. If you feel like you hasten to figure things out by yourself because you lack faith, I encourage you to ask God to increase your faith. This is the same request the disciples made to Jesus during his earthly ministry.

3. When you have faith in God, you are willing to wait upon Him. To wait is one of the hardest things to do, especially when you are on verge of losing something you value.

4. Our possession is heaven and our hope is in heaven. Christianity survived under furious kings and rulers who tried to wipe out the entire Christian scriptures and religion just because it is the work of God Himself. Our confidence in Him, and through Him in the future, makes Christianity a unique faith and lifestyle.

5. When we get caught in worldly worries, we tend to depend on our instinct and worldly resources. If you are in such a situation, the word of God encourages you to surrender all before God, that He may start working to fix your life and situation. Your surrender before Him is your victory over the problems, worries and temptations in the world.

6. Did you receive Christ because you thought accepting Him as Lord and Savior was going to fix everything? I am sorry, Beloved, if you have not experienced such worldly joy. Trust in the Lord and He will direct your path. You need to remember God's promises are for good, and you have to have confidence in them that they will come to pass in your lifetime.

7. Remember the role model of faith, Abraham, who never got to enjoy the fulfillment of promises made to him in his lifetime; but each promise came to pass. Jacob died with the same promise, while Moses saw the Promised Land but never got to enter!

8. If you consider your confidence (in your walk with God) stronger than those men of faith I have just mentioned, then you may question why you have not seen the fulfillment of God's promises in your life so far. If you are to become more like Christ, then remember that Christ suffered, but His confidence in the hope of resurrection brought Him back to life and proved Him to be the promised Messiah

Nightly Activity

The Nightly Activity is designed to track the productivity of your everyday life to analyze how the 31 day journey is helping you to become a better person and a better leader. It also serves as a journal. As you advance in your journey, you should look back every day and constantly check the nightly activity page to see whether you are improving. Circle a number you consider to be the overall productivity level of your day. Color the circle you consider to be your spiritual growth level today. See Appendix I.

I observed:_____

_____

I learned:_____

_____

I changed:_____

_____

Review of the day:_____

_____

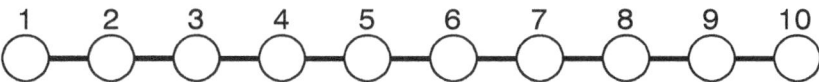

Day 10

WALKING BY FAITH:
Confidence in Our Strength or God's?

I f you are walking by faith, you just can't have confidence in your own strength. It's like you can't hate someone if you love them. Realistically speaking, confidence in the future and in unseen things seems very absurd to the human mind. Cerebral knowledge and understanding will never capture the full picture of God's grace and His presence in our lives; consequently, it will not allow us to follow unseen evidence of spiritual realities. The supernatural intervention of God's sovereignty in our life surpasses all the knowledge and understanding of man. Your confidence can either be in you, or in God.

Not too long ago I applied for a position and the interview went really well. The interviewers seemed very godly people. The job title, hours, salary and the description was very good too. The job was in a seminary, so working in a Christian environment and getting paid would have been ideal. After the interview, I felt very confident based on the interest of the interviewers and our mutual understanding of the job description. I felt so confident that I built my hopes so high; I had not even a hint of a doubt that I would get the job. My confidence in my education, experience, talents, and public relations was not the only the thing which removed all sort of doubts: it was my humbleness before God; I prayed, I fasted. It seems I was confident of my physical and spiritual abilities. I waited and waited because I was supposed to get a phone call from human resources regarding the hiring. Eventually, I lost patience after a few days and gave a follow up call. The man was not on the phone. I felt my confidence was shaking now, but then I said to myself, "You are the best candidate for this job, you have a doctorate degree in the required field, and you have prayed and fasted. God is not going to disappoint you."

Regardless of all the confidence, somehow a new movement inside of me was on the rise. I started feeling the effects of "what if…?" "What if" shook the very foundation of my confidence, and within an hour, I felt so disappointed and distressed that I called my fiancé to tell her I didn't know if I would get the job. Now the mighty confidence was shredded into tiny pieces. I had not even received any word on the interview, but inside of me I lost the fight. I lost my confidence, and now even if the news would be negative, it would not cause any damage. The real damage was made with the simple assumption that I would not get the job. Finally, one day I received a message on my answering machine saying, "You were a very good candidate, but we decided to go with another candidate." I called back and asked the reason. I was told, "You were over-qualified." Wow! Can a man over-qualify for something? This was the first question I asked, while I broke down before God. I needed that job, and I had prayed, fasted, and probably had the best education anyone could have had for that job. "You over-qualify" got stuck with me. I applied to a number of other places and ended up getting nothing. Oh, wait a minute … I did get something: disappointment and lack of confidence in the American education system. I started pondering, what is this over-qualification? In the cooperative world there are many ways to explain, but in the spiritual realm there is only one way to explain. I was over-confident, just like the Jews in Jesus' day. They were confident that they would receive the heavenly kingdom, because they belonged to Abraham. They were confident of their lineage,

Word of Encouragement

"And this I pray, that your love may abound still more and more in real knowledge and all discernment, so that you may approve the things that are excellent, in order to be sincere and blameless until the day of Christ." (Philippians 1:9-10)

and their over-confidence made them arrogant. God had to send them into captivity to teach them. Jesus admonished them in their over-confident behavior, because they were mistaken. I was over-confident about my spiritual efforts. I needed a blow in the face to remind me that I had crossed the line.

Remember in Heb.11.1, confidence is used as an adjective to clarify and emphasize what kind of assurance we need to have in the hope to qualify for one who has faith.

In my above experience, I learned a number of things but by and large, the most significant thing I discovered was my confidence was in myself as opposed to God. Sometimes we overlook that, especially when it comes to ministry and church leadership. We tend to replace God-confidence with self-confidence, because whatever we are doing is related to God's work. So there are times when we listen to our mind and heart rather than God's Heart and Mind. Thus we pray and fast, yet we lose. Maybe in those times we need to reevaluate our relationship with God. We may need to check our motives and the foundation of our confidence often to see if Christ is the focus of our lives, or if we have replaced Christ with ourselves. We need to remind ourselves that, "In whom [Christ] we have access to God in boldness and confidence through faith in him" (Eph.3:12).

Hebrews 1:11 starts this definition with two words: confident assurance. I believe such assurance in the hope for the future and unseen things comes from the Holy Spirit, the supernatural source. Paul says, "But each of us was given grace according to the measure of Christ's gift" (Eph.4:7 ESV). Therefore, no matter what you do, some have more faith than others. I like the passage of Scripture where the disciples ask Jesus to increase their faith (Luke 17:5). Can faith be increased? Yes, indeed. I have experienced such an increase, simply by walking by faith and asking Him to increase my faith.

Now, I would warn you when you ask God to increase your faith, it does not happen like a miracle or magic, but it is a slow process which may require long periods of trials, suffering, and persecution with faithful obedience to Him. You may find yourself whining, disliking and even hating what may happen in your life, but remember the example of Job. Even Abraham had to come to a point where he had complained, cried, and even disliked obeying God when he took Isaac to sacrifice. But just at the time when he was about to slaughter his son, God found him faithful and provided a ram for him. His walk with God is a prime example of faith.

In the summer of 2004, I decided to follow God's command and visit Afghanistan and Iran. Previously, in the spring of 2003, God had exposed me to a whole new level of faith by bringing two young men to Christ from another major monotheist religion. This encouraged me to go and minister to Afghanis and Iranis. So, in 2004 I set off on an unknown journey. My mission agency in the USA didn't give me any financial, spiritual or emotional support, apart from my mentor and spiritual father, who always encouraged me to follow what God asks me to do. My family in Pakistan was also not happy and certainly did not want me to travel to Afghanistan or Iran, particularly since I did not have any money or any connections in those countries.

The journey itself was an extraordinary blessing; on my way I met many Muslims and got to share my faith. I came across death a number of times, but God never allowed anything to harm me. I was often pushed by the Holy Spirit to leave one place and to move to another—just a few hours before bomb attacks or fights took place. I could see the hand of God upon me, and to me it was a once in a lifetime experience and absolutely uplifting. I saw the Sovereign God holding me, a sinner, in His hand, and moving me from one place to another, yet using me as a clean vessel for His glory among gentiles. I had never gained a more confident assurance in that which we hope is going to happen until I took this Journey with Him. Through the will of God and under the influence of the Holy Spirit, I knew what would happen next. Still today, I look back at that experience to get a spiritual boost to get done what God has called me to do in New York City. When you do not have finances or other resources to fulfill God's call for you, don't be deceived, just start walking in the direction God has asked you to go, and He will provide everything you need. It may not be what you want, but it's certainly something you need. When God called Abraham out of the land of his father to follow Him, Abraham did not question, he just followed. If God desires to give you all sort of worldly riches He will, but if He wants to glorify His name from the nothing you have, He will do that also. I love the story of Gideon; he was hesitant of his call at first, but when he knew it was not from his own desperate desire to see the salvation of his nation, he did not doubt when God decided to glorify His own name. Gideon had 22,000 fighting men, a very little army for a huge enemy, yet God took only 300 out of those 22,000 to bring victory to Israel! God alone is able to shape a person like Gideon into a courageous warrior and leader.

Step 10 toward becoming a better leader is to be assured of the confidence we have in God; that He can turn ordinary people into extraordinary people. His sovereignty can make you into a mighty leader, even if you have nothing, and nobody knows you. But first, you need to understand the difference between your confidence in yourself and your confidence in God. Also you need to determine the line separating confidence from over-confidence, or risk losing everything.

Questions and Comments of Day 10

1. Do you rely on your own strength, or is God your power and strength?

2. Without Christ we are nothing, so being nothing we can't make any right decision. Therefore, if God has made a decision for your life and He has revealed it to you through various sources-you had better follow.

3. Never think that you know all and you have all the answers just because you have been a Christian for your whole life. God speaks in quietness, so take time and pray to Him. Spend some more time trying to understand exactly what He wants you to do. Walking with God and having confidence in your own strength proves that you are not walking by faith at all.

4. You may think that you are walking by faith while you believe in your own strength. But on the last day you will be told, "I don't even know you." Please leave your every decision, major or minor, for Him to make.

5. Do you get suspicious when God asks you to do something, questioning whether it is God or your own thoughts? If you do, welcome to the valley of being human. As a human we all wrestle with this question.

6. Do you look for the resources first, when God calls you? Or do you act with faith that He will provide? Either way, you need to spend more time in prayer than in planning and figuring out the details.

7. What bothers you the most when you are leading a group? Is it the lack of confidence of people in you, or your lack of confidence in people?

8. Who are you trying to please: people, yourself, or God?

9. What do you think about your hope in the future that you have in Christ? Are you certain enough in that hope that you can bear the tough tests of faith?

Nightly Activity

The Nightly Activity is designed to track the productivity of your everyday life to analyze how the 31 day journey is helping you to become a better person and a better leader. It also serves as a journal. As you advance in your journey, you should look back every day and constantly check the nightly activity page to see whether you are improving. Circle a number you consider to be the overall productivity level of your day. Color the circle you consider to be your spiritual growth level today. See Appendix I.

I observed:_____

_____

I learned:_____

_____

I changed:_____

_____

Review of the day:_____

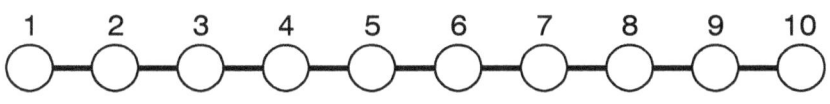

_____

```
 1    2    3    4    5    6    7    8    9   10
 O----O----O----O----O----O----O----O----O----O
```

WALKING BY FAITH:
Persecution

Heb.10:32-33 is a classic example of the confident assurance of believers who wrote the history of the Church, "But recall those earlier days when after you had been enlightened, you endured a hard struggle with sufferings, sometimes being publically exposed to abuse and persecution, and sometimes being partners with those so treated. For you had compassion for those who were in prison and you cheerfully accepted the plundering of your possessions, knowing that you yourselves possessed something better and more lasting." This was something that Jesus foretold during his ministry on earth. He said in Luke 20:12, 16 & 17, "...they will arrest you and persecute you; they will hand you over to synagogues and prisons and you will be brought before kings and governors because of my name...you will be betrayed, even by parents and brothers, by relatives and friends, and they will put some of you to death, you will be hated by all because of my name." In verse 13, Jesus explains the importance of such persecution and the results it will produce. He continued, "This will give you an opportunity to testify. So make up your mind not to prepare your defense in advance; for I will give you words and a wisdom that none of your opponents will be able to withstand or contradict." The result of our endurance does not end at this stage, but verses 18 and 19 say, "But not a hair of your head will perish. By your endurance you will gain your souls."

It is the confident assurance in hope that inspires Christians in persecuted areas of this world to be persistent and never give up. To me, leaving mother, father, brother and sister behind was a difficult step. It was painful leaving for a journey where you don't even know if you will live or die, but the confident assurance in hope kept me strong. Jesus said, "Whoever loves father or mother more than me is not worthy of me; and whoever loves son or daughter more than me is not worthy of me; and whoever does not take up the cross and follow me is not worthy of me" (Matt.10:37-38). I have experienced the truthfulness of Jesus' promise that "those who find their life will lose it, and those who lose their life for my sake will find it" (Matt.10:39).

Word of Encouragement

Polycarp sat at the feet of the Apostle John. History tells us that he was the bishop of Smyrna. According to Ruth Tucker, in A.D 156 anti-Christian persecution broke out in the province of Asia. This is where it was suggested to Polycarp, "why, what harm is there in saying, Caesar is Lord?" When he was asked to deny Christ, Polycarp replied no because of the Hope he had in Him. The civil authorities burned him alive.[3] Jesus says, "Do no fear what you are about to suffer. Behold, the devil is about to cast some of you into prison, that you may be tested, and you will have tribulation for ten days. Be faithful until death, and I will give you the Crown of life" (Revelation 2:10).

Worldly leaders throw their followers into danger to save themselves and their family's lives. But Christian leaders are supposed to give their lives for their followers. Jesus said that a good shepherd gives his life for his sheep. We declare our first love for God when we love Him more than any other relationship. Our declaration hurts Satan like a sharp knife. And when he can't win us back by tempting us, he makes unfair and difficult circumstances that cause Christian followers to lose their confidence in God.

Discouragement is the first demon that may enter into the congregation, or a group, during the wave of persecution. I remember when two of the church members at my father's church back home got shot. Both survived, but they were approached with money and other attractive proposals to leave my dad because he was not able to help them with medication and their family's everyday needs.

If you do not have confident assurance, you need to confess before God and let Him work in your life. Be prepared for the next wave of persecution. One of the biggest factors that becomes a hindrance in developing confident assurance in hope is fearing the devil. The Bible teaches about two types of fears. One is a healthy fear and the other is not. A kind of fear we have for our older siblings or parents, where we love them and respect them, but also fear them, is an example of a healthy fear. This we should have for God, out of our love and reverence for Him. The Bible teaches, "The fear of the Lord is the beginning of knowledge" (Psalm 111:10). Such fear is required in order to gain knowledge of not only the seen world, but also the unseen realities. The other type of fear is the dangerous one, and that is the fear of losing possessions, family, friends, and even one's life. Jesus said, "Do not fear those who kill the body but cannot kill the soul; rather fear him who can destroy both soul and body in hell" (Matt.10.28).

Step 11 towards becoming a better leader depends on your confident assurance in the work of Christ in your life and in your ministry. Your leadership will improve radically if you are confident that nothing can damage even a single hair, unless God allows it. So let the Lord be your confidence and assurance in every way of your life.

Questions and Comments of Day 11

1. If you have lost someone because of persecution, be encouraged that their sacrifice was not in vain. God will bring His justice.

2. If you are being persecuted or discriminated against, I want you to remember that God said, "vengeance is mine" (Deuteronomy 32:35).

3. Have peace, because your reward in heaven is great.

4. If you are afraid because the enemy is strong and you see no way to defeat him, just pray and God will deliver you.

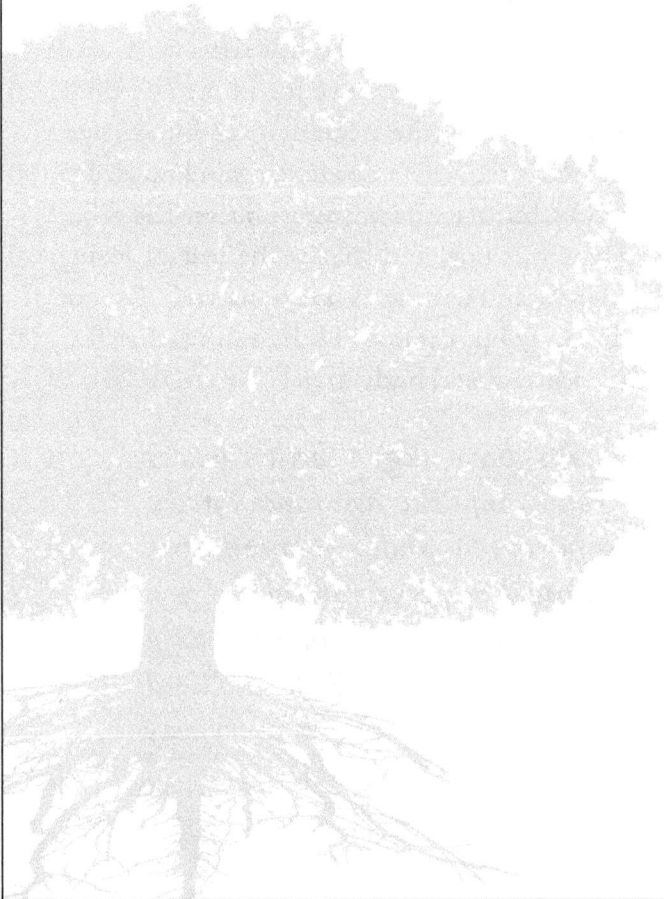

Nightly Activity

The Nightly Activity is designed to track the productivity of your everyday life to analyze how the 31 day journey is helping you to become a better person and a better leader. It also serves as a journal. As you advance in your journey, you should look back every day and constantly check the nightly activity page to see whether you are improving. Circle a number you consider to be the overall productivity level of your day. Color the circle you consider to be your spiritual growth level today. See Appendix I.

I observed:_____

_____

I learned:_____

_____

I changed:_____

_____

Review of the day:_____

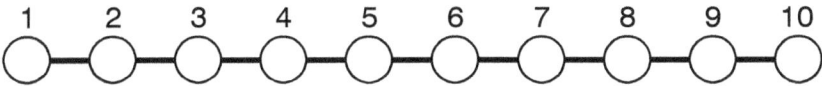

_____

1	2	3	4	5	6	7	8	9	10
O	O	O	O	O	O	O	O	O	O

WALKING BY FAITH:
Hope

A story has been told about a certain Indian soldier who was employed by the East India Company. He was sent into the battlefield. Many died; he lost his closest friends, with whom he had grown up in a small village. One of his childhood friends died in his hands. While he was pulling him back to bury him with respect, a bullet hit him in his right arm, and another passed through his body (entering through the back and passing through the front). It damaged his backbone, and consequently paralyzed him. This half-dead soldier suddenly imagined himself with his newlywed wife back in his own beautiful small village. For a minute he thought he was dead, and then he heard the sound of shooting. He realized that recalling those memories reduced his pain, so he let himself slip into his happy memories.

He thought about how, every day in the mornings his father goes to the field long before others wake up. The field made him think about the greenery in his village; he thought of the harvest and it reminded him of the freshly baked flat bread with dasigee (cooking grease). These thoughts generated hope in him to see his village again; to spend the rest of his life with his newlywed wife and grow old with her. He desired to get up early and check on the field like his father, and to bring comfort to the lives of his parents. His hope gave him courage to hold on. In a few hours medical help arrived, and he was taken into a tent where an English doctor operated on him, and after taking the bullets out they bandaged him. Now, every day he saw people dying on his right and left, but he kept his mind on the past good memories and continued thinking about the village.

If a man is walking in darkness and he sees a very tiny light up somewhere ahead of him, he will be willing to walk an extra mile to get there. Hope is something which keeps every individual fighting to survive. In Christianity, hope has deeper meanings. The early church was strong in faith, since they had fixed their eyes on the reward in heaven. The early church was encouraged by Scriptures such as, "We can rejoice, too, when we run into problems and trials, for we know that they help us develop endurance. Endurance develops strength of character, and character strengthens our confident hope of salvation, and this hope will not lead to disappointment.

For we know how dearly God loves us, because he has given us the Holy Spirit to fill our hearts with his love" (Rom. 5:3-5 ESV). I like how (in Romans chapter 5) Paul

Word of Encouragement

Paul writes, "For God has not given us a spirit of timidity, but of power and love and discipline. Therefore do not be ashamed of the testimony about our Lord, or of me His prisoner; but join with me in suffering for the gospel according to the power of God who has saved us, and called us with a holy calling, not according to our works, but according to His own purpose and grace which was granted us in Christ Jesus from all eternity." (2 Timothy 1:7-9)

presents a full picture of Heb 11:1, in v.1 and v.2b. Both talk about faith, how God has brought us to faith. It's not ourselves who can claim any credit for having faith in God, but God himself takes the initiative and fills us with faith, that we may believe in

Christ. Our sinful nature cannot and will not allow us to start the process of faith. When a person is dead physically, he can't move: it must be an external force, coming in contact with the dead body, to make it move. Spiritually we died when Sin entered the world; thus Adam's sin brought death into the world, and to our spiritual state of life. Of course, physical death was just a physical evidence of spiritual reality; "so death spread to everyone for everyone sinned" (Rom.5:12 ESV).

Therefore, how can a spiritually dead person move his/her spiritually dead body, unless by the mercies of God you are given faith to believe in Christ's work of salvation. Paul emphasizes in v.2a that our faith in Christ has made peace between God and us so that His wrath may not consume us. The second part of the same verse starts breaking down the definition of faith, as it is described in Heb.11:1. The word Paul uses in the second half of the second verse is "confidence." Paul encourages the poor, persecuted church to be thankful for their trials and suffering because it is bringing them close to God.

As human beings, many times we complain and blame God for everything that goes wrong in our lives. When the unrighteous enjoy the riches of this world and rejoice in their blessings, it makes us believers a little uncomfortable and we seek justice before God. Justice before God may not satisfy the limited and filthy desires of humanity's sinful heart. Psalm 7:11-15 says, "God is a righteous judge, and a God who feels indignation every day. If a man does not repent, God will whet his sword; he has bent and readied his bow; he has prepared for him his deadly weapons, making his arrows fiery shafts. Behold, the wicked man conceives evil and is pregnant with mischief and gives birth to lies. He makes a pit, digging it out, and falls into the hole that he has made" (ESV).

Step 12 towards becoming a better leader is to have hope, even when it seems the world is against you and circumstances are getting worse. Have peace and confidence in the hope you have in Christ, that He will come through.

Questions and Comments of Day 12

1. As a leader, you need to be hopeful that God will direct your path, and that you will able to lead. If you are facing any crisis, remember Jesus says, 'hold on little longer.'

2. If you lose your hope-what will your followers and those who look up to you do?

3. Hope in Jesus will get you through even the most deadly experience!

4. To those who walk by faith, hope never dies; so if you are walking by faith, your hope is the confirmation of your faith in Him.

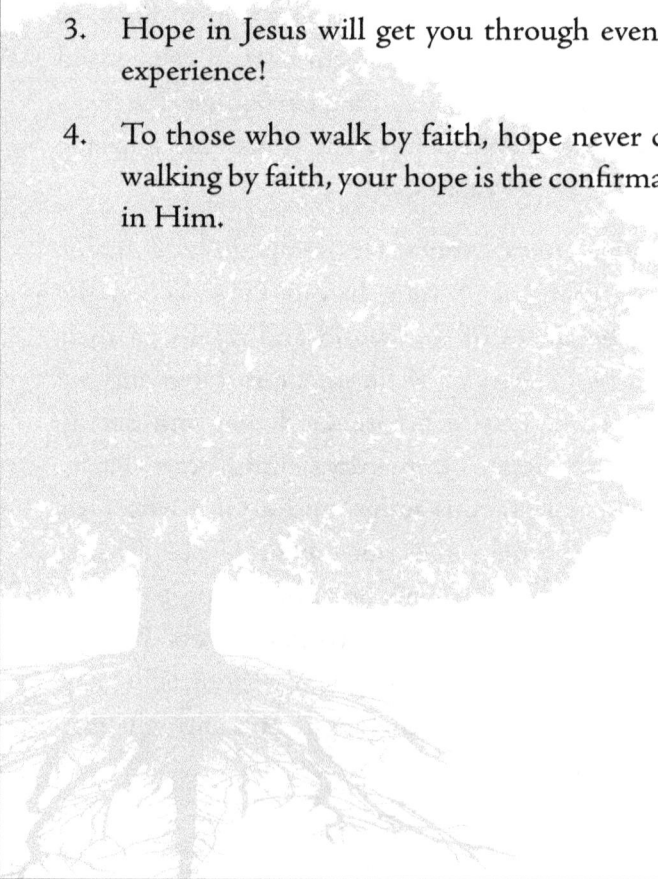

Nightly Activity

The Nightly Activity is designed to track the productivity of your everyday life to analyze how the 31 day journey is helping you to become a better person and a better leader. It also serves as a journal. As you advance in your journey, you should look back every day and constantly check the nightly activity page to see whether you are improving. Circle a number you consider to be the overall productivity level of your day. Color the circle you consider to be your spiritual growth level today. See Appendix I.

I observed:_____

_____

I learned:_____

_____

I changed:_____

_____

Review of the day:_____

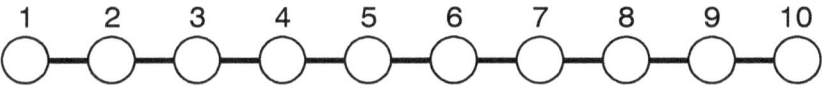

_____

1   2   3   4   5   6   7   8   9   10
O—O—O—O—O—O—O—O—O—O

Day 13

WALKING BY FAITH:
Boldness

There are a few qualities Christianity has received as an inheritance from the apostles and the early church. One of them is boldness. A true follower of Christ is a person who is bold in his faith and actions. Sometimes we encounter leaders who are not bold, but are very good at their jobs. You may have seen some of these leaders in your church, organizations, or even in the government. When you look at them, or hear them speaking, you question—what in the world happened to the people who elected or selected that person? When we think about a leader, we imagine a person who is tall, eloquent, brave and bold. When God asked Moses to go and tell Pharaoh to let his people go, Moses was very nervous. At first, he refused to go because he was not eloquent in speaking. In the end, however, God used him mightily. I don't know about the exact height of Jesus Christ, but I know from the scripture that He was very eloquent, brave and bold. This is true in the lives of the apostles too. They were not afraid of anyone when it came to speaking the truth. They were not breaking the law or doing anything wrong, yet they were considered traitors because of their unwillingness to accept what is wrong. Their boldness inspired many to take a stand for what is right. At the same time many turned against them because it exposed their filthiness, craftiness and hypocrisy.

I also find Paul to be a very bold leader among the early church leaders. As a matter of fact, I consider him to be my hero. He was bold in his faith, in speech, in character and in witnessing. His boldness was a unique combination of love for the gentiles, and an eagerness to see the Lord. He writes, "as it is my eager expectation and hope that I will not be at all ashamed, but that with full courage, now as always, Christ will be honored in my body, whether by life or by death" (Philippians 1:20 ESV). In Acts 13:46, "And Paul and Barnabas spoke out boldly, saying, 'It was necessary that the word of God be spoken first to you. Since you thrust it aside and judge yourselves unworthy of eternal life, behold, we are turning to the Gentiles.'" Paul's boldness got him into trouble with the government and with church leaders; but this was the same boldness for which he received respect. His boldness encouraged him to be fearless. Just like when Jesus was going to Jerusalem and told His disciples that He would be handed over to the authorities, Paul also knew his time was coming; but he was bold even to the end of his life.

> ## Word of Encouragement
>
> *Following Polycarp's death, Justin was one of the early church Christians whose boldness cost him his life … but left an everlasting impression. He followed the Platonic school of philosophy, which he used to intelligently present Christianity. After Justin's martyrdom he has been referred to as Justin Martyr for his boldness.*

Both Jesus and Paul (as well as all the apostles and many early church leaders) knew what their boldness would cost them. They found life nothing compared to the joy they were experiencing in the hope for eternal life. One small step could have saved their lives, but they were bold about their faith to the point of death. Paul encouraged the believers, "What are you doing, weeping and breaking my heart? For I am ready, not only to be imprisoned, but even to die in Jerusalem for the Name of the Lord Jesus" (Acts 21:13 ESV).

Boldness means saying 'yes' for yes, and 'no' for no. I know from personal experience that boldness in Christ may not necessarily make you popular with others, but it will set an example for some. You may be persecuted for your boldness, but Christ told us during his early ministry that we will be persecuted for the sake of His name. People may turn against you because of your boldness in Christ, but in the end you will be victorious. It is because of this boldness of the early church that we have the scriptures today. It was due to the boldness of some that today we experience freedom and democracy in most of the world.

My future father-in-law is a senior pastor in upstate New York; he has been in ministry for thirty years. Once he was sharing a story about when he and his friend went to audition for a drama production at a junior college. They went in and were given scripts, which contained profanity and inappropriate language. He was very proud and encouraged by his friend, who looked at the script and, disregarding his desire to act, told the director and crew that he is a Christian and can't use such language. He was dismissed right away, but he definitely left an everlasting mark on my future father-in-law's life and probably on others who were there. Your boldness may cost you something and you may not be able to see the positive results, but in the presence of God you will be considered a hero. This joy is greater than any cost.

Many times we lose the opportunity to reach out to someone just because we are not bold enough in our faith. I regret some of the times when I should have been more bold in witnessing; however, my regrets make me stronger for any future opportunity. God knows what He is doing, and how He is using us to enhance His kingdom. He is able to see the full picture. Our boldness in Him and for Him gives us an opportunity to become a part of that picture. If a leader is not bold, most likely he will not have many followers and those he does have will be lukewarm. Jesus said in Revelation, "So, because you are lukewarm, and neither hot nor cold, I will spit you out of my mouth" (Rev 3:16 ESV).

Jesus said, "Do not fear what you are about to suffer. Behold, the devil is about to throw some of you into prison, that you may be tested, and for ten days you will have tribulation. Be faithful unto death, and I will give you the crown of life" (Rev 2:10 ESV).

Step 13 toward becoming a better leader is simply be bold in your faith, decisions, character and speech.

Questions and Comments of Day 13

1. Do you think you are bold enough that, even if you had to give your life, you would? I know many Christians think they will, but when it comes to practical application, it is very hard.

2. Put yourself in Queen Esther's place and see if you would dare to take the same step she took, knowing that she could be killed for her action. Her boldness saved the whole Jewish nation.

3. What if you are told to tone down your teaching. Will you continue sharing the truth of the scriptures with the same boldness, or will you bring it down to a comfortable level for others?

4. What would you do if the government banned church services and forbid Christianity? Would you risk your life and continue worshipping God underground, as is the custom in many other countries—or you will stop going to church?

Nightly Activity

The Nightly Activity is designed to track the productivity of your everyday life to analyze how the 31 day journey is helping you to become a better person and a better leader. It also serves as a journal. As you advance in your journey, you should look back every day and constantly check the nightly activity page to see whether you are improving. Circle a number you consider to be the overall productivity level of your day. Color the circle you consider to be your spiritual growth level today. See Appendix I.

I observed:_____

_____

I learned:_____

_____

I changed:_____

_____

Review of the day:_____

_____

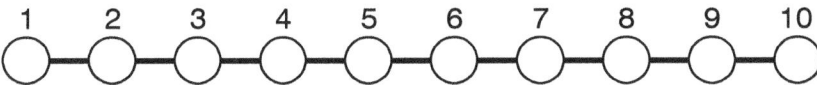

1   2   3   4   5   6   7   8   9   10

WALKING BY FAITH:
Perseverance

I n the early 1970s, a man decided to follow Christ. One day as he was passing by a colony and saw the land and the inhabitants, a desire was born in his heart. The desire turned into a vision. From then on, every time he passed by the colony he lifted his right hand toward the colony and prayed for the land. His vision was to have a church in that place. There was no church on the land because it was actually military ground. He continued praying for that piece of land for years. Ten years passed by with no answer from God, yet he continued praying the same way. Every time he passed by, he lifted his right hand and prayed for a place of worship. After 15 years, an old friend came to visit this man of God and share about an opportunity. He told the man about an investment. The man was very excited because the investment was in the same land about which he had been praying for the past 15 years. He didn't have money, but he knew that if it was from God that He was going to provide. Today there is a beautiful church building in that colony that the man was diligently praying for, and a strong church congregation. This man was the founder of this church and is still the senior pastor. How do I know? Because I am his son.

If I have learned one thing from my father, it is perseverance. When he sets his heart on something, he waits and waits and eventually God provides. Since day one, many attacks and threats have been aimed at him, but none have shaken his faith. Jesus told a story about an unjust judge who was not paying attention to the request of an old woman. The woman was perseverant; she kept asking for justice. Finally the unjust judge had to provide for her needs because she was bugging him. Through this, Jesus was showing how much more the Just Father will do for those who are persistent in their requests. When you are walking by faith, you need perseverance. Paul teaches in his letter to the church of Ephesians, "[pray] at all times in the Spirit, with all prayer and supplication. To that end, keep alert with all perseverance, making supplication for all the saints," (Eph 6:18 ESV).

An exemplary leader never gives up, remaining focused on his vision. If you have been entrusted with a vision and you know that it is for God's glory, never give up! Continue praying, fasting, and sharing your vision with others. What is impossible for God? Nothing! If you trust and worship the God of the impossible, then wait a little longer and He will provide. Remove the statement, "God doesn't listen to me," from your life.

Word of Encouragement

Paul was a perseverant servant; he endured almost every type of persecution and hardships you can ever imagine, and today we gain insight from his writing when it comes to ministry and leadership. He writes, "Three times I was beaten with rods, once I was stoned, three times I was shipwrecked, I spent a night and a day in the open sea, I have been constantly on the move. I have been in danger from rivers, in danger from bandits, in danger from my own countrymen, in danger from Gentiles, in danger in the city, in danger in the country, in danger at sea; and in danger from false brothers. I have labored and toiled and have often gone without sleep; I have known hunger and thirst and have often gone without food; I have been cold and naked. Besides everything else, I face daily the pressure of my concern for all the churches." (2 Cor. 11:25-28)

He does listen to you. The story of Daniel is another excellent example of perseverance. He prayed to God and the answer took twenty one days but he didn't give up. Daniel 10:12-13 says, "Then he said to me, 'Fear not, Daniel, for from the first day that you set your heart to understand and humbled yourself before your God, your words have been heard, and I have come because of your words. The prince of the kingdom of Persia withstood me twenty-one days, but Michael, one of the chief princes, came to help me, for I was left there with the kings of Persia.'"

It may take some time before you receive the result of your prayers-but it will come. Your perseverance is essential for faith and the victory of the Lord's armies. When you start losing heart, you let Satan rejoice in you. The ultimate goal of Satan is to keep you away from trusting God. He will do whatever he can; either he will hurt you, or someone dear to you, or when he can't do much else, he will try to block your prayers in the spiritual realm.

Step 14 towards becoming a better leader is to hold on to your faith. Be perseverant, and you will be victorious.

Questions and Comments of Day 14

1. If there are complications in your leadership that you have been praying about, trust in the Lord that your answer is about to come to you.

2. Do not let the forces of darkness discourage you; be persistent and diligent in your prayers. Whatever troubles you are going through, God is about to remove them. He has already sent His archangel to protect and encourage you.

3. You are already victorious! Do not let the enemy whisper in your ear that God will not answer your prayer.

4. God has chosen you to be his servant, and He has called you by name to be a leader; therefore, go and be courageous!

5. Remember, nothing is impossible for our Sovereign God.

6. Have peace and confidence that your prayers have been answered. Wait a little longer and you will see the result of your perseverance.

Nightly Activity

The Nightly Activity is designed to track the productivity of your everyday life to analyze how the 31 day journey is helping you to become a better person and a better leader. It also serves as a journal. As you advance in your journey, you should look back every day and constantly check the nightly activity page to see whether you are improving. Circle a number you consider to be the overall productivity level of your day. Color the circle you consider to be your spiritual growth level today. See Appendix I.

I observed:_____

_____

I learned:_____

_____

I changed:_____

_____

Review of the day:_____

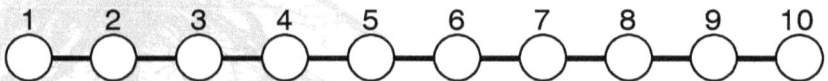

_____

1 2 3 4 5 6 7 8 9 10

Day 15

WALKING BY FAITH:
Investment

In 1999, when I was still in my home country, I invested some money in a business. At first it felt like a deceptive business, but then I was assured that the people who were working there were Christians. I immediately trusted them. To make a long story short, I lost of all my money because of such trust in this poor investment. Since then, when people try to pull the, "we are Christian, they are Christians," card, I feel that they are trying to manipulate me. If you are a Christian, you don't need to tell people that to gain their trust. People will trust you, because they will see your character. It was a good thing that God taught me this lesson because when I came to the United States, on three different occasions some very good Christians asked me to join them for a similar kind of business. You may know the term, "Multilevel Marketing," when you buy a product (your investment in the company), then market it so other people will invest. When they get others to invest as well, you get a share of everyone's profit and investment. Personally, I have not known of even one person getting richer by those kinds of businesses, though there are many stories which I consider to be marketing stunts.

My point is this: when you invest your money, time, energy and relationships, you have to make sure the investment is worthwhile. Your investments toward both physical and spiritual worlds need to be measured on the scale of eternal outcomes.

The Bible teaches us to store our treasure in heaven; it also tells us to use our earthly possessions for the glory of God. If we are entrusted with anything, we need to be careful where we are investing it. Your investments of time, money and energy are the most significant things you can invest in any area of your life, but your most important investment should be in your relationships. I have witnessed many leaders both Christian and secular who are talented and hard-working. The outcome of their leadership always resulted in financial gain, a boost in the productivity of the organization, a dramatic increase in the number of congregations, and many other positive things. I have also witnessed their personal and family lives. They lost the battle at home because they did not invest in their relationships. It is also true with our relationship with God. The Bible testifies, "For what shall it profit a man, if he shall gain the whole world, and lose his own soul?" (Mark 8:36 KJB). The bottom line is that working late nights, planning and strategizing for upcoming events and daily meetings perhaps bring growth to your ministry/organization, but it will not improve your personal relationship with God and your family.

In the Bible, there is one statement that scares me more than any other verse: "I do not know you." Matthew 25:1-12 describes a parable of ten virgins. It says five were wise and five were foolish. Five wise virgins entered in the bridegroom's party because they were ready, but the five who were foolish couldn't enter because they were not ready. When the hour came, they were supposed to be ready; however, by the time

Word of Encouragement

"Listen, my beloved brethren: did not God choose the poor of this world to be rich in faith and heirs of the kingdom which He promised to those who love Him?" (James 2:5)

they got ready, the door was already closed! The problem in the parable is not time, money, or energy. It is about relationships. Because all ten were invited, they received the same invitation. I assume somehow they knew the bridegroom, but apparently the bridegroom did not know five of them.

The Scriptures say, "Afterward the other virgins came also, saying, 'Lord, lord, open to us.' But he answered, 'Truly, I say to you, I do not know you,' (Matthew 25:11-12). Let's look at the story step by step. So all ten were invited; all ten were excited for the party (investment of energy); all ten were waiting (investment of time) for the bridegroom. I am sure that all ten had bought nice clothes for the wedding (investment of money), but five were wise enough to invest in the relationship too.

The bridegroom knew them, but the others never established a personal relationship with him. You may know the president of your country, and if someone tells you that the president is coming into the town, I bet you will invest your time in waiting for him; you will invest your money to buy nice, presentable clothes, and invest your energy staying up and alert, because you don't want to miss his arrival. But here is the issue: you may know him, but he doesn't know you. (It's similar with movie and sports stars). Unless we invest in our relationship with God, all our other investments are worthless! The day when Christ arrives, He may tell us, "I do not know you." I would be so crushed.

Although the statement "I do not know you" sounds very cold and unlike our sweet, loving, caring and merciful Jesus, it's true.

Step 15 *towards becoming a better leader is to invest wisely, both spiritually and physically.*

Questions and Comments of Day 15:

1. As you become more like Christ, you can know better where to invest your time, energy, and money in relationships.

2. God wants us to be wise in every way of our life, especially when we are leading people.

3. Which of these aspects of your life (spending time, making money, using energy, and developing relationships) are the most significant to you? How do you invest in them?

4. Visualize these four aspects of your life (spending time, using energy, making money, and developing relationships) as commodities and chart where each one is prioritized in your life? Which one is first, second, third, and fourth? Please draw a chart, to make it easier to account for your stewardship of them.

5. Developing your relationships, and stewarding your time should go hand in hand; money should be last. Using your energy, should be almost as high as using your time, and developing your relationships, I would encourage you to change the order of your investments every week to see which investment is bringing more productivity in your personal and spiritual life. Start with Comment number 4 and then try number 5, and a few other combinations and note the differences.

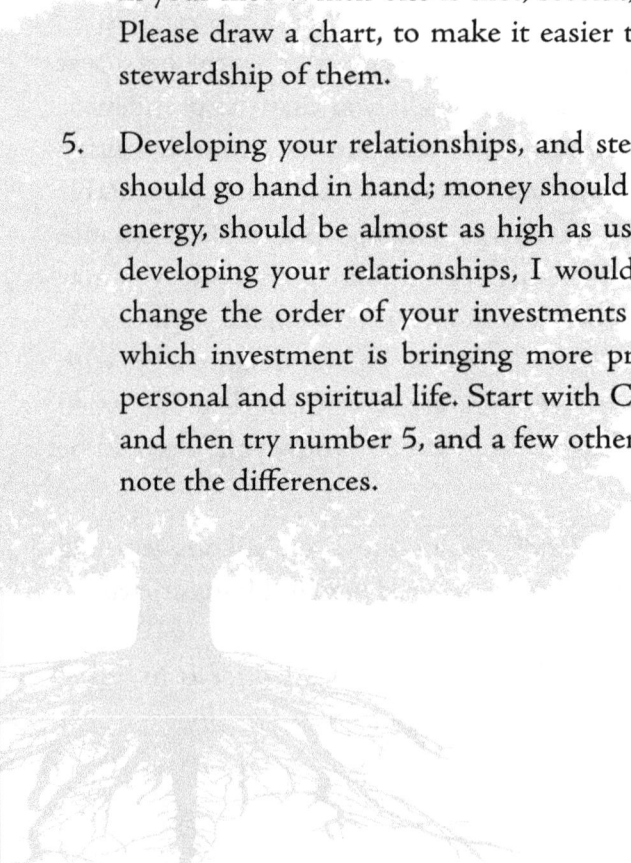

Nightly Activity

The Nightly Activity is designed to track the productivity of your everyday life to analyze how the 31 day journey is helping you to become a better person and a better leader. It also serves as a journal. As you advance in your journey, you should look back every day and constantly check the nightly activity page to see whether you are improving. Circle a number you consider to be the overall productivity level of your day. Color the circle you consider to be your spiritual growth level today. See Appendix I.

I observed:_____

_____

I learned:_____

_____

I changed:_____

_____

Review of the day:_____

_____

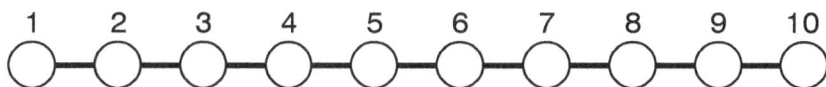

1   2   3   4   5   6   7   8   9   10

Day 16

WALKING BY FAITH:
Productivity

Early spring weather is always pleasant and breath-taking in Wayne, Pennsylvania. It was about the end of spring in Wayne when I was exposed to another aspect of walking by faith; this unique aspect is the productivity of our lives. I was a minister in an independent church in Trappe, Pennsylvania (about 40 minutes outside of one of the most famous cities in America, Philadelphia). I felt deep in my spirit that something was wrong with my spiritual walk with the Lord. I started fasting quite often. I was putting 70-80 hours into my work each week. My church leaders were concerned about my life, fearing that I would get burned out if I did not slow down. The senior pastor spoke to me on several occasions saying that I needed to take off, "go for a vacation or something." No one was able to understand what was wrong with me—not even I, myself.

Later at the end of summer, I found myself receiving a clear sign from God that I was not being productive. My productivity was not real. I was a pastor, but reaching out to the local church congregation was not my calling. I felt that God had called me to be a missionary—not a pastor. My soul was thirsty to see the fruit of outreach and evangelism, but instead, I was involved in shepherding one particular congregation. It is hard to understand whether or not you are productive when you are doing God's ministry and things are going pretty smoothly. I remember I once told a group of young Christian men and women that it is hard to choose between good and good, compared to choosing between good and evil. I guess each one of us gets to an intersection where we pause to see if we are heading in the right direction. Our walk with God by faith needs to be very productive. If we have spent most of the years of our life doing what God has not called us to do, yet it has brought glory to His name, souls have been saved, and a difference has been made in the lives of sinners and believers, still our soul will remain thirsty for the productivity that is uniquely the result of God's special calling.

Word of Encouragement

The world may consider your investment and your ways foolish, but remember what the Scriptures say: "Because the foolishness of God is wiser than man, and the weakness of God is stronger than men. For consider your calling, brethren, that there were not many wise according to the flesh, not many mighty, not many noble; but God has chosen the foolish things of the world to shame the wise and God has chosen the weak things of the world to shame the things which are strong."
(1 Corinthians 1: 25-27)

Speaking of the call, let me ask you. Do you know what you are called to do? What is it that God wants you to contribute to His Kingdom? Are your spiritual gifts being used in the right place, or you are just targeting anything and everything? You need to be precise when it comes to ministry. Paul gives a caution to Christians: don't "punch the air" (I Corinthians 9:26). If our energy and efforts are not focused on what God wants us to do, then we are not building His Kingdom. We are just pretending to be one of the participants who are working in the field. It's like the other day, when a bunch of people were moving a table into a worship place and I saw a brother touching the table. He said, "Well, at least I am pretending to be working." Have you heard people asking you a simple question in a sarcastic way?

"Are you working hard, or hardly working?" Most of us are inclined to work when we have to, but if we grasp the idea of productivity, we may able to understand what true productivity really means. It means you use your investments of either your time, energy, money or relationships for a greater purpose. What if that brother who was touching the table really lifted it up, using his energy and time? Why not push a little harder and get it done? He would be dividing the weight, reducing the total time and energy consumption, and more than anything else, he will really be a part of the group, the beginning of building relationships. Productivity of an individual is as important as the productivity of the whole group. An unorganized team or group can't accomplish anything besides arguments and confrontations. Disagreements are inevitable in a group where individuals refuse to use the full potential of their investment. In contrast, organized people or groups can be crucial members of a community, just because of the level of their productivity. If you are focusing on "walking by faith" but you are not productive, I am sorry to say, you are not building His kingdom; rather you are distracting others who are doing their part of the work. In a worldly organization such a person would not be welcome. However, in church such a person receives grace.

In Christ you can't stand in one place. You have to move forward, and if you are not moving forward, then you are moving backward. Jesus' earthly ministry was always moving forward, and the disciples learned to move quickly because they saw their leader being productive in His walk with God. Walking by faith is not only waiting upon God and letting Him work in our lives, but it is also using the gifts of salvation and life wisely for His Kingdom. Jesus asked His father in heaven to bless His disciples, and those who would come to faith by hearing the message of salvation through them. In Matthew 25, He told a parable of talents. In the parable, the master punished the one who didn't earn anything. Mat 25:25-28 says, "'so I was afraid, and I went and hid your talent in the ground. Here you have what is yours.' But his master answered him, 'You wicked and slothful servant! You knew that I reap where I have not sown and gather where I scattered no seed? Then you ought to have invested my money with the bankers, and at my coming, I should have received what was my own with interest. So take the talent from him and give it to him who has the ten talents.'" In verse 30 the master ordered, "And cast the worthless servant into the outer darkness. In that place, there will be weeping and gnashing of teeth."

Step 16 *towards becoming a better leader is to be productive in every area of your life.*

Questions and Comments of Day 16

1. Do you analyze your level of productivity? If not, here is a chance for you start. Such an analysis will help you to determine where you are heading with your investments in the Kingdom of God. Do it biweekly, monthly and yearly.

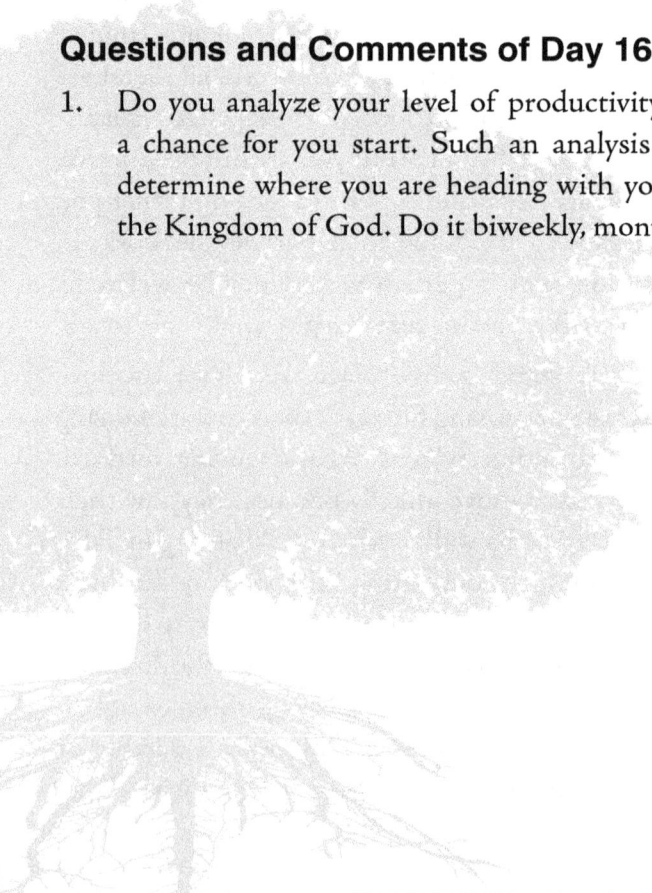

Nightly Activity

The Nightly Activity is designed to track the productivity of your everyday life to analyze how the 31 day journey is helping you to become a better person and a better leader. It also serves as a journal. As you advance in your journey, you should look back every day and constantly check the nightly activity page to see whether you are improving. Circle a number you consider to be the overall productivity level of your day. Color the circle you consider to be your spiritual growth level today. See Appendix I.

I observed:_____

_____

I learned:_____

_____

I changed:_____

_____

Review of the day:_____

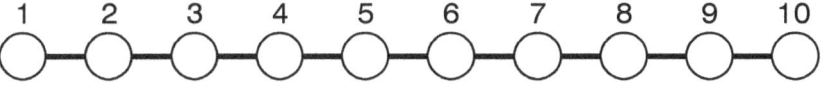

_____

1   2   3   4   5   6   7   8   9   10
O—O—O—O—O—O—O—O—O—O

Day 17

WALKING BY FAITH:
Effectiveness

The analysis of your productivity takes you to the next level of becoming a better leader, and that is the effectiveness of your work and leadership. Peter Drucker, one of the best-known and most widely influential thinkers and writers on the subject of management theory, predicted that information will bring major changes in society. He argued that "knowledge has become the central, key resource that knows no geography. According to him, the largest working group will become what he termed 'Knowledge workers.'" In his book The Effective Executive, he writes, "Every knowledge worker in modern organization is an "executive" if, by virtue of his position or knowledge, he is responsible for a contribution that materially affects the capacity of the organization to perform and to obtain results.⁴" According to him, whether a chief executive or beginner, he or she needs to be effective. He writes, "Effectiveness can be learned.⁵" He appeals to executives, knowledge workers, managers, or individual professionals, who are expected (by virtue of their position or their knowledge) to make decisions in the normal course of their work that will have a significant impact on the performance and results of the whole. In his book *Practicing Greatness: 7 Disciplines of Extraordinary Spiritual Leaders*, Reggie McNeal presents a biblical worldview regarding such leadership. He talks about key events

---

4 Drucker, *The Effective Executive*
5 Drucker, *The Effective Executive*

in a person's life that make him an effective or ineffective leader. According to McNeal, "Key events may be positive or negative: significant encounters with God, separation or divorce of parents, death of a loved one, a great achievement, an educational milestone, a move to another part of the country or world, a failed marriage, being fired, or enduring a major conflict in ministry are just a few examples.[6]" Drucker states that the key words in the process of learning effectiveness are "knowledge worker," "quality," "decision making," "results," and "responsibility for his or her contribution.[7]"

The knowledge workers cannot be supervised or helped, but they must direct themselves toward improving performance and a contribution toward effectiveness. If you think about becoming more effective, then stop thinking and do it. Effective leaders' motivation depends on their being effective, and on their being able to achieve. Drucker also mentions, "Intelligence, imagination, and knowledge are essential resources, but only effectiveness converts them into results.[8]" It is essential for a Christian to be an effective worker. McNeal writes, "All leaders have a dark side, because every human being struggles with dysfunction to some degree. The dark sides of leaders are just more noticeable (to others more often than to themselves, un-fortunately) because of the public scrutiny they receive and because of how their implications are amplified through their followers.[9]" He provides a list of the types of dark side leaders: compulsive, narcissistic, paranoid, co-dependent, and passive-aggressive.

If you are a leader, then you need to remember that people are watching you. I heard from a leader that he had never recognized his gift of leadership until the day when a mother invited him for supper. (He was serving in a church as a youth pastor during those days.)

---

6 McNeal, *Practicing Greatness*
7 Drucker, *The Effective Executive*
8 Drucker, *The Effective Executive*
9 McNeal, *Practicing Greatness*

Word of Encouragement

"For the word of the cross is to those who are perishing foolishness, but to us who are being saved it is the power of God." (1 Corinthians 1: 25-27)

While they were eating, the mother told him that her son had been watching him every day and she was so thankful for his character, because her son looked up to him. The young pastor never even noticed her son much in youth group. It was a wake-up call for the pastor, and from that day on the youth pastor started taking his leadership even more seriously. It certainly does not matter who you see when you are around people; it's the people who see you and determine what kind of influence you are. Sometimes we overlook our responsibilities and leadership role. We think our role is so minor that it will not make any difference if it is effective or not. We tend to believe nobody is going to notice, but there is always someone. It's like this: a while back my car's air conditioner broke. My fiancé took it to a mechanic and they spent so much time looking for the problem. Eventually when they found it, it did not even take ten seconds to fix it because it was a little tiny part which was unhooked.

The point is, little minor roles we overlook or think are not important are still essential parts of the body of Christ: the Church.

A very small book in the Bible, actually it's a one chapter letter from Paul and Timothy to Philemon, reveals the truth of effectiveness. It says, "and I pray that the sharing of your faith may become effective for the full knowledge of every good thing that is in us for the sake of Christ" (Phm.1:6 ESV). He also talks about an opportunity he is considering for an effective work of ministry. To the church of Corinth he writes the following words, "for a wide door for effective work has opened to me, and there are many adversaries" (1Co 16:9 ESV). As servants of God, we are required to do effective work. Don't be afraid of adversaries, because when you are walking by faith, those mountains of adversaries will become flat ground for you. Christian leaders need to look at the usage of their time, and ask themselves constantly whether they are using time effectively. Christ used his every hour of ministry on earth effectively, to set a model for us to follow.

> *Step 17 toward becoming a better leader is to be an effective worker.*

Questions and Comments of Day 17

1. Whether you think you are a leader or not, remember you will be influencing at least ten thousand people in your lifetime. It is up to you what kind of influence you want to have.

2. No Christian or leader can sustain themselves without being effective.

3. Do you consider yourself a "knowledge worker"? What about the quality of your personal and church life?

4. When you make decisions, do you put Christ in the midst of the decision-making process?

5. What are the results of your ministry, leadership or life as a Christian?

6. Do you believe that you are responsible to contribute to the body of Christ?

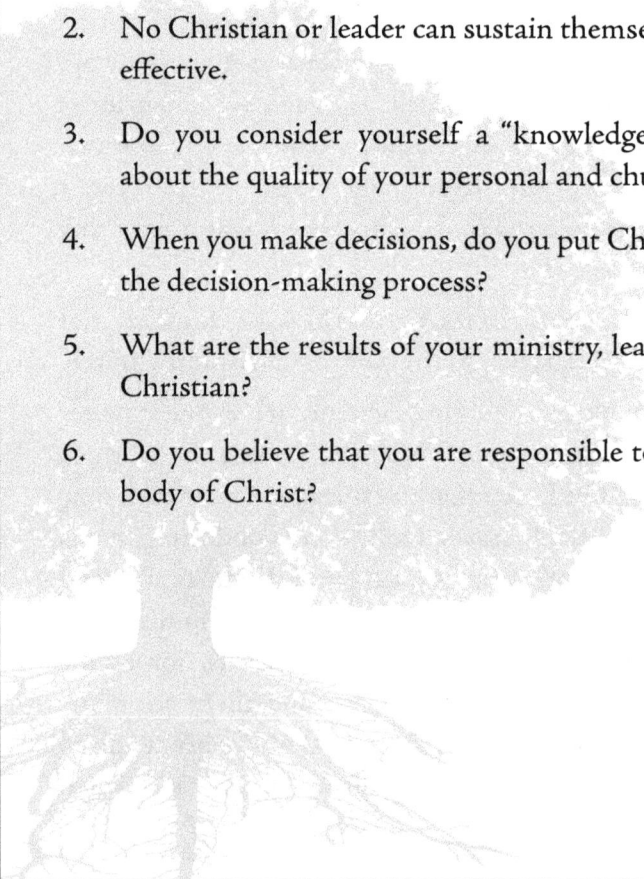

Nightly Activity

The Nightly Activity is designed to track the productivity of your everyday life to analyze how the 31 day journey is helping you to become a better person and a better leader. It also serves as a journal. As you advance in your journey, you should look back every day and constantly check the nightly activity page to see whether you are improving. Circle a number you consider to be the overall productivity level of your day. Color the circle you consider to be your spiritual growth level today. See Appendix I.

I observed:_____

_____

I learned:_____

_____

I changed:_____

_____

Review of the day:_____

_____

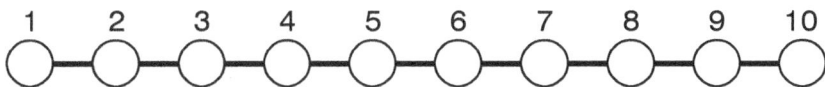

WALKING BY FAITH:
Changing Agent

To attain more effectiveness, you may need to change a few things around, even within your own leadership style. Executives can be defined as captives of the organization. They are forced to keep on operating, unless they take positive action to change the reality in which they live and work. An executive is an agent of change. If the executives are hesitant to change, then most likely they will be driven by adverse circumstances. In other words, the reality around them and the flow of events will determine what they are concerned with and what they will do about it. If a leader is hesitant to change, "He may be an excellent man, but he is certain to waste his knowledge and ability and to throw away what little effectiveness he might have achieved.[10]" Therefore, executives of organizations are expected to acquire the ability to get the right things done. Executives also need to remember that leadership is not about controlling others, but it is about enabling them to act. Their deeds are far more important than their words.

Jim Kouzes and Barry Posner identify some of the crucial characteristics of an effective leader in their book, The Leadership Challenge: How to Get Extraordinary Things Done in Organizations. They say that traditional management teaches us that leaders ought to be cool, aloof, and analytical-separating

---

10 Drucker, *The Effective Executive*

emotion from work. Yet when leaders discuss the things they are proudest of in their own careers, they describe feelings of inspiration, passion, elation, intensity, challenge, caring, kindness, even love[11]. Don't you think that the secular world is realizing that an effective leader must use his emotions? Kouzes and Posner point out some of the following:

- Effective leaders are involved and in touch with those they lead.

- They care deeply about others, and they often refer to those with whom they work as family.

- Leadership is not a place, it is a process.

- Leadership is disciplined passion.

- Leadership begins where management ends, where the systems of rewards and punishments, control, and scrutiny, give way to innovation, individual character, and the courage of convictions.

Change happens when leaders lead with character—when they are honest, competent, forward-looking, and inspiring. Kouzes and Posner found in their research that there are five practices common to most extraordinary leadership achievements.

- They challenge.
- They inspire.
- They enable.
- They model.
- They encourage.[12]

It is inevitable that the people under a manager can be executives or leaders due to their effectiveness, regardless of their limited

---

11 Kouzes and Posner, *The Leadership Challenge*
12 Kouzes and Posner, *The Leadership Challenge*

Word of Encouragement

Jesus said, "I am the resurrection and the life. He who believes in me will live, even though he dies, and whoever lives and believes in me will never die. Do you believe this?" (John 11:25-26)

resources and authority. They do not depend on managing people. They are focused on their ability to change, and to contribute towards the progress of an organization through their effective work and decisions. In the process of learning effectiveness, it is very crucial to understand what is meant by knowledge work. We talked briefly about it previously. Knowledge work is not defined by quantity or costs, but by its results.

An individual market researcher with knowledge and vision can be equally productive, without staff, as a manager who has many people working in market research. Such a manager may be so busy managing that there is no time for market research or for fundamental decisions. In his lecture to doctoral students at Liberty University, Dr. Daniel MacMillan, the former president of Bluefield College, shared about his personal experiences in the early years of his appointment as the president. According to him, the president's role is as a changing agent. Strategic planning is important for the progress of an educational institution, but more than that, it is the values, belief, and mission of the institution which play vital roles in the progress of any organization. When he took the position of president, there was a need for sound management and sound financial guidance. He made himself approachable to everyone for the improvement of the college. He suggests that, to bring change for the better, there is a need to understand the college context. It is important to know who comes to college, where they are from, what their family backgrounds are, and what their church backgrounds are. If they want to continue their jobs, they need to be effective leaders. Leaders need to understand the values and beliefs of the people with whom they work. The same rule applies to ministries and churches. You must know your congregation on a personal level. Recently I heard about a pastor who has started a new movement in his church after a few deaths in his congregation. The deaths were caused by heart disease, high blood pressure, diabetes, and other such problems. The movement was on a personal level. The pastor and church together were holding each other accountable for what they eat, and if they exercise. It brought the people of the church so close that they were one.

Dr. Ron Ingle, the former president of Coastal Carolina University, once stated in his lecture at Liberty University that people are not naturally anti-change. He described change as an act of imagination. He emphasized that imagination is not like a fairy tale, but something which must be dealt with. Another important factor for change is to have a budget plan, especially if someone spends much effort to plan but does not know how to pay for a particular project. Planning and budgeting have to be integrated. It is necessary to locate revenue sources. He recommends a complete assessment and a feasibility study before any new change in organization.

As leaders of ministries and churches, we should be careful with our planning. God has given us the responsibility, and He will hold us responsible if something goes wrong because of our decision. Let the Holy Spirit make your decision. In order to do that, you need to spend more time on your knees praying and fasting than in sitting around a table planning. Nevertheless, assessments and feasibility studies are crucial for any organization.

Step 18 towards becoming a better leader is to be bold in your decisions. If you know the Holy Spirit is asking you to make certain changes in the organization, do not be afraid. You are the changing agent.

Questions and Comments of Day 18

1. As a leader, how much time do you spend thinking about the effectiveness of the ministry, and how much time do you spend in prayer and fasting?

2. Do you think you need a change, and are you, or your followers, afraid of change?

Nightly Activity

The Nightly Activity is designed to track the productivity of your everyday life to analyze how the 31 day journey is helping you to become a better person and a better leader. It also serves as a journal. As you advance in your journey, you should look back every day and constantly check the nightly activity page to see whether you are improving. Circle a number you consider to be the overall productivity level of your day. Color the circle you consider to be your spiritual growth level today. See Appendix I.

I observed:_____

_____

I learned:_____

_____

I changed:_____

_____

Review of the day:_____

_____

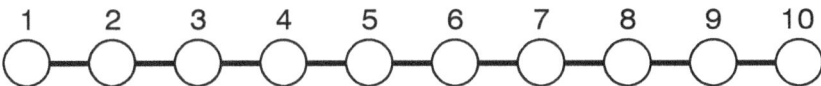

1   2   3   4   5   6   7   8   9   10

WALKING BY FAITH:
God's Ways

This world has separated its ways from God's ways. What is right in the eye of this world does not fit with the pattern of God's ways. Leadership is God's own attribute. When we read Genesis, we are comforted with God's intentions to bless man with leadership. Genesis 1:26 says, "Then God said: 'Let Us make man in Our image, after Our likeness. Let them have dominion over the fish of the sea, the birds of the air, and the cattle, and over all the wild animals and all the creatures that crawl on the ground.'"

The history of Israel is full of the concept of leadership. God brought up good leaders and rejected bad leaders. For a long time, until the people of Israel demanded a king, God was their political, religious, social and economic leader. The world never wants to change its ways; therefore, the natural tendency of the average person in this world is to stay where he or she is. God's way of leadership is full of changes, and He encourages those whom He puts into positions to lead groups of people, either organizations or nations, to bring positive change. If someone wants to be a leader, then the person should be ready for change. Why Change Doesn't Work, by Harvey Robbins and Michael Finley, was published in 1997. According to this book, there are two laws of change: push and pull. The law of push is that people do what they perceive to be in their best interest, while the law of pull is that people are not inherently anti-change.[13] Change in an organization is very stressful; nevertheless, stress can be a very important factor in accomplishing goals. When someone wants to bring change in an organization, he'd better have a good reason and a solid plan. The only way to bring change that lasts in an organization is to visualize what a leader wants to accomplish.

> ## Word of Encouragement
>
> *"Who shall separate us from the love of Christ? Shall tribulation, or distress, or persecution, or famine, or nakedness, or peril, or sword? Just as it is written, 'for thy sake we are being put to death all day long; we were considered as sheep to be slaughtered.' But in all these things we overwhelmingly conquer through Him who loved us." (Romans 8:35-37)*

We need to rely on God more than on any other thing. Degrees are good for knowledge, but true knowledge comes from God. When Solomon was asked what he wanted, he asked for wisdom and knowledge. Aubrey Malphurs provides four instruments (or indicators) to assess the effectiveness of our leadership in our ministries. The list of these instruments is as follows: a spiritual gifts inventory, a temperament indicator, a leadership role indicator, and a natural gifts and talents inventory[14] (I strongly recommend taking Aubrey Malphurs' assessment test). Knowing about your spiritual gifts, identifying your temperament, understanding your leadership role, and your natural gifts and talents can help a leader to be transformed into a person who can successfully lead a nation or an organization. Your spiritual gifts and natural gifts may overlap at times, and other times they may contradict; however, your temperament is very crucial in your leadership. It can scare people away or bring them close to you. I personally do not want to see a person with mood swings like a rollercoaster.

---

13 Robin and Finley, *Why Change Doesn't Work*
14 Malphurs, *Maximizing Your Effectiveness*

I can't work in an environment where people are hot tempered and always arguing and yelling.

God wants us to be gentle in our spirit and talk so that people may see Christ in us. If you are a hot tempered person and you cannot control yourself, you should step down from your position and let the Lord heal you fully. I would recommend prayer, fasting and the book of Proverbs. Proverbs 17:2 says, "It is better to be a wise slave than a foolish son." Leadership is not about position but empowerment; it includes consistency, choices, credit, character, and credibility. Proverbs 17:7 says, "Fine speech is not becoming to a fool; still less is false speech to a prince." If the leader is honest, most likely the organization will earn a good reputation and the staff will be honest too. Proverbs 15:2 says, "The tongue of the wise uses knowledge rightly, but the mouth of fools pours forth foolishness." A wise and good leader uses his tongue very carefully.

The biblical way of leadership is the best way of leadership. When we put God before ourselves, when we as leaders trust in Him to lead us so we may lead others, He guides us. In His leadership there is no mistake. He is perfect, and He wants us to rely on Him for our needs. He is the author of our destiny. Wisdom comes from Him, and He blesses people and chooses them to lead people and nations. Leaders practice God-given authority to lead and guide a group of people toward their destiny. Therefore, it is important for a leader to understand his/her spiritual gifts in order to lead others efficiently to the right path. Dependency on God and faith in His promises can enable a Christian leader to get through rough times without losing any members or followers.

Step 19 towards becoming a better leader is to follow God's way, even if it means to go against the world, and the social norms of a culture.

Questions and Comments of Day 19

1. Do you make your decisions based on what God wants you to do, or on what people want?

2. Are you a people pleaser or a people saver? Would you let a person go to hell because you want to be nice and not offend him or her, or would you speak the truth of the Scripture even if it hit him or her like bullet?

3. God's ways are different than the ways of man. Man is rebellious towards God, and the only Hope for a man is Christ. When Christ comes into our lives, He transforms us into new beings that are able to adopt God's ways to live our lives.

4. As a Christian leader, are you struggling with following patterns of God's way?

Nightly Activity

The Nightly Activity is designed to track the productivity of your everyday life to analyze how the 31 day journey is helping you to become a better person and a better leader. It also serves as a journal. As you advance in your journey, you should look back every day and constantly check the nightly activity page to see whether you are improving. Circle a number you consider to be the overall productivity level of your day. Color the circle you consider to be your spiritual growth level today. See Appendix I.

I observed:_____

_____

I learned:_____

_____

I changed:_____

_____

Review of the day:_____

_____

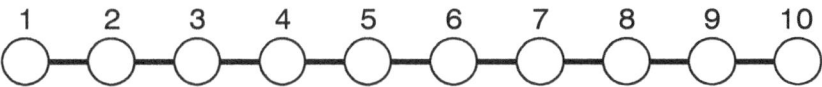

1   2   3   4   5   6   7   8   9   10

WALKING BY FAITH:
Influence and Your Worldview

John C. Maxwell, an internationally recognized leadership expert, speaker, and author, has sold over 12 million books. His organization has trained more than one million leaders worldwide. He writes in his book, *Developing the Leader Within You*, that the key to success in any endeavor is the ability to lead others successfully[15]. Also in his book *Leading from the Lockers,* he made a profound statement, that you "make a difference tomorrow by becoming a better leader today.[16]" The Great Commission, in Matthew 28:19-21, has made all of us missionaries, evangelists and leaders. Once we become Christians, we should desire to tell others about Christ. The joy of salvation is so immense that a human body, mind and soul just can't contain it. It starts pouring out through our speech, character and actions. When this happens, people want to follow us. Therefore, it is important to learn how we can become better leaders today, to make a difference tomorrow.

Yesterday we talked briefly about influence and how you will influence others. Now it is up to you whether to be a positive influence or a negative one. Let's ask the Holy Spirit to make us a positive influence on those who are around us.

---

15 Maxwell, *Developing the Leader Within You*
16 Maxwell, *Leading from the Lockers*

About ten years ago, I saw an anti-cigarette commercial on TV. In the commercial, a dad is reading a book in his living room and he is writing or underlining something on the pages of the book. Nearby, his three- or four-year-old son is sitting playing with toys. He sees his father and observes for a while what he is doing. The child gets a colored pencil and starts squiggling on a piece of paper. Just like his dad, he begins scratching his head, putting the pencil under his teeth, and trying to move

Word of Encouragement

"Blessed be the God and Father of our Lord Jesus Christ, who according to His great mercy has caused us to be born again to a living hope through the resurrection of Jesus Christ from the dead, to obtain an inheritance which is imperishable and undefiled and will not fade away, reserved in heaven for you, who are protected by the power of God through faith for a salvation ready to be revealed in the last time."
(1 Peter 1: 3-5)

it between his fingers. Then the child notices that his dad takes a cigarette and lights it to smoke. The child does the same with his color pencil. The dad did not notice because he had his book in front of his face. There are times when we influence negatively or positively without knowing it. People around you may imitate you. Your influence will leave a lasting impression on many lives.

During three and a half years of His ministry, Jesus influenced his disciples. They were with him all the time. 2 Corinthians 10 talks about influences. One of the verses says, "We do not boast beyond limit in the labors of others. But our hope is that as your faith increases, our area of influence among you may be greatly enlarged" (vs.15 ESV). There are people you are influencing, and then there are people who are influencing you. If your walk with God is influenced by Scripture, I assure you that you will be a positive influence for others and will not be disappointed. But if influenced by a person, remember people are imperfect; therefore, they are capable of disappointing you. No matter what area of ministry you are serving in or leading, you need to look around and see who is influencing you and who you are influencing.

The Spirit of God encourages us to 'go make disciples,' and the process of disciple making will not be effective if we are not influencing positively. True discipleship begins with positive influence; if discipleship could be done by teaching, then the Bible schools and seminaries would have won this whole world. Discipleship is not academia or occasional lectures or sermons. Discipleship is impacting someone's life by what you say and do. Your everyday life makes disciples. You influence your community, starting with your own home. If your family considers you a positive influence within the family, that is a really good start to knowing how the community you live in will think about you and how you would influence them. If I had to define leadership, I would say it is the direct influence of a person and how he or she makes people follow him or her. If people are willing to follow you because you are a model Christian, then you are a leader. True leadership is not a position given in return for a salary because of your academic credentials, knowledge and personality; but it is when people follow you because they want to. Jesus was not hired, but He was followed; Paul, Peter and other apostles were not hired, but followed. Many secular leaders were not hired for the job, but they were followed.

There are many areas of influence. As a leader, it is your responsibility to make sure that you know in what areas you are weak. Where do you have to improve your influence?

Your influence is also subject to your personal worldview. According to the Oxford English[17] Dictionary, worldview means, "contemplation of the world" and a "view of life." There is always a clash between the worldview of this world and Christianity. Jesus'

---

17 *Oxford English Dictionary*, Edition 1989

worldview was different than the religious leaders of His time, and also different from the government. Therefore, Jesus influenced the world differently than other leaders (whether religious or political). According to Mark Cosgrove, "A worldview is a set of assumptions, or presuppositions, that are generally unconsciously held, but affect how we think and live. A worldview is a set of important beliefs that normally we inherit unthinkingly from our academic and cultural ancestors.[18]"

A Christian worldview finds its base in the absolute God, who is all-powerful and almighty. He has put certain characteristics in man which cannot be ignored. These characteristics are ethics and values, but the corrupt nature of man has manipulated the truth; therefore the law functions so that everything may stay in order. The law of the land and the law of the Holy Scripture both are important for Christians, particularly if you are a leader. Jay Budziszewski writes:

> "The difference should not be overstated. Are people completely ignorant of the moral character of chastity? Probably not. Even today, most people involved in sexual sin recognize its impurity more clearly than they let on. But they may not see the depth of the problem. An element of honest ignorance mingles with the element of denial, and God's revelation does more than admonish us that we know better. It corrects the error, steadies the wandering judgment, and imparts certainty.[19]"

What you do, and how you perceive things, all depend on your worldview. Christians are supposed to develop their worldview on the basis of the Scriptures. If your worldview is truly biblical, then you will love your enemy regardless of how

18 Cosgrove, *Foundations of Christian Thought*
19 Budziszewski, *"Natural Law Revealed."*

they treat you, you will be obedient to your government, and you will do the Will of God on this earth.

According to George Barna, "A biblical worldview is a means of experiencing, interpreting, and responding to reality in light of biblical perspective. This view provides a personal understanding of every idea, opportunity, and experience based on identification and application of relevant biblical principles so that each choice we make may be consistent with God's principles and commands.[20]" God has called you to be a leader, and He wants you to develop your worldview on the fundamental beliefs of Christianity. Don't follow the world, because that worldview will corrupt your mind and encourage you to rebel against God.

> **Step 20** *towards becoming a better leader is to develop excellent traits, so people want to follow you-not because you are hired for the job, but because you have influence. Also, evaluate your worldview; is it biblical? If not, you may need to work on your worldview first.*

Questions and Comments of Day 20

1. Check around and see how many people you have influenced, then compare it to how many people have influenced you. This influence could be minor or major, positive or negative. It would be a good exercise to evaluate your impact on others.

2. Pick a few people (maybe two or three) and deliberately try to be involved in their lives. See by the end of month (or year) how you have influenced their lives.

---

20 Barna, *Think Like Jesus*

3. Ask your family members if you are a positive or a negative influence. Ask them to be honest with you. If they bring up some dark areas of your influence, please consider working on those areas as your first priority.

4. If you are a student, think about the students you have not spoken with, or asked their opinion.

5. It's never too late to correct your mistakes. If you know that your worldview is based on traditions and on the expectations of this world, then you may need to start all over again. Start studying the word of God. I recommend the book of Romans.

6. Your worldview about life, the world, Christianity, ministry and God are significant.

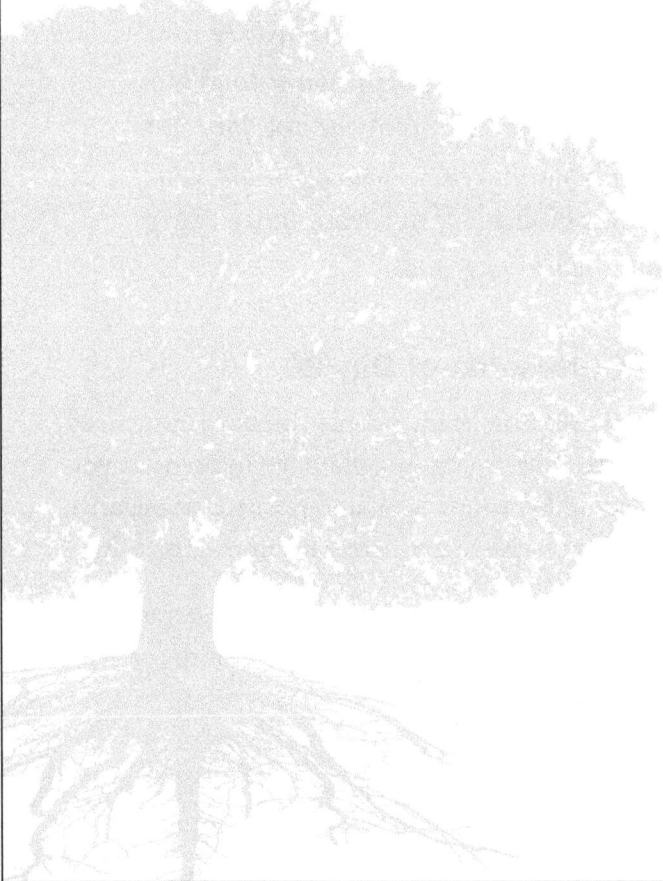

Nightly Activity

The Nightly Activity is designed to track the productivity of your everyday life to analyze how the 31 day journey is helping you to become a better person and a better leader. It also serves as a journal. As you advance in your journey, you should look back every day and constantly check the nightly activity page to see whether you are improving. Circle a number you consider to be the overall productivity level of your day. Color the circle you consider to be your spiritual growth level today. See Appendix I.

I observed:_____

_____

I learned:_____

_____

I changed:_____

_____

Review of the day:_____

_____

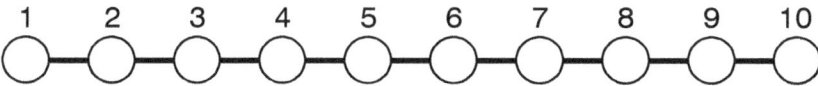

| 1 | 2 | 3 | 4 | 5 | 6 | 7 | 8 | 9 | 10 |

WALKING BY FAITH:
Leadership Style

A leadership style is the manner in which a leader leads a team or group of people. All the precious steps toward becoming a better leader lead to refining your leadership style. Your worldview about life, people, the world, Christianity, ministry and God play a critical role in developing a leadership style. Your leadership style is a process of social influences that build up a team of followers who can envision that vision of the leader to make or do something extraordinary. It is the ability of a leader to integrate and maximize available manpower and resources to accomplish a common task. According to Dr. Ann Marie E. McSwain, an Assistant Professor at Lincoln University, "Leadership is about capacity: the capacity of leaders to listen and observe, to use their expertise as a starting point to encourage dialogue between all levels of decision-making, to establish processes and transparency in decision-making, to articulate their own values and visions clearly but not impose them. Leadership is about setting and not just reacting to agendas, identifying problems, and initiating change that makes for substantial improvement rather than managing change.[21]" The motivation is usually considered intrinsic (part of the essential nature of someone or something) when individuals perceive themselves to have control

---

21 *"Food for Thought: Memorable Quotes."*

over environmental factors and over their own behavior. Behavior is motivated by both intrinsic and extrinsic (not part of the essential nature of someone or something and operating from outside) factors. A Christian leader needs to pay attention to extrinsic factors in order to create an environment in which a follower's intrinsic motivation may be released, and then to guide and sustain that motivation.

Word of Encouragement

"For we also once were foolish ourselves, disobedient, deceived, enslaved to various lusts and pleasures, spending our life in malice and envy, hateful, hating one another. But when the kindness of God our Savior and His love for mankind appeared, He saved us, not on the basis of deeds which we have done in righteousness, but according to His mercy." (Titus 3:3-5a)

Howard M. Carlisle clearly states that motivation is largely the responsibility of the managers and administrators. He writes, "Motivation includes the internal state plus all the other internal and external factors that determine the amount of energy and enthusiasm an individual puts into a job… Motivation in this sense is viewed as a management activity.[22]" In order to achieve the central objective of integrating faith and learning, it is essential to decentralize administrative functions and actively encourage everyone in the team to participate in decision-making and in the overall management of the ministry.

The bottom line is to follow the principles of God's truth and to stay under the guidance of He who is the repository and the instigator of all knowledge. This motivation cannot be achieved without increasing satisfaction and reducing dissatisfaction of a person who is anticipated to follow the pattern of God's truth. The idea of God's supreme power has become so unrealistic to

---

22 Carlisle, *Management*, 211

the new generation in the West that the pattern of God's truth seems unacceptable to society. The biblical leadership style is the pattern of God's truth. Christ Himself, in his physical body demonstrated the leadership style as a servant leader. Today, Christ being the perfect model motivates the church to rely on God in both good times and bad times. If our decision-making ability remains under the authority of God, then we will certainly accomplish the task and fulfill the vision. Paul encourages the church, "And I am sure of this, that he who began a good work in you will bring it to completion at the day of Jesus Christ" (Phil 1:6 ESV). As a Christian leader, your leadership style should prove the sovereignty of God and the truth of His scripture.

Your leadership style is again something which you can figure out by asking those people who are honest with you and would like to see you improving your leadership. The other way is adopting. Adopt a leadership style you find the most interesting and closest to your spiritual gifts. When I teach leadership courses, I always encourage students to read the life of a number of leaders, specifically biblical leaders, and to draw a character sketch of some of the leaders. I encourage them to make a list of their traits (either positive or negative) and examine what biblical characters they can identify with as a leader. Think about what characteristics you prefer to have, and then work hard to become like the one leader you consider to have the best leadership style. It may sound cliché, but I always try to model Jesus' leadership, who is the supreme model of servanthood leadership. You will be surprised how fast you will learn from copying and adopting His style of leadership.

Step 21 towards becoming a better leader is to find out your leadership style.

Questions and Comments of Day 21

1. Have you ever seen a person who would like to be Hitler, or who liked his leadership style? If you go around and ask people for good leaders, they will tell you the name of a person who was humble, meek, gentle, loving, caring, and had many other good qualities. The point is that people like a leader who they can come before without hesitation.

2. Cultural values have great influence in the mediation process of leadership style. Your motivation may vary from others.

3. Personal values determine the values of a society and a nation.[23]

4. Your education may play a very tiny part, but your practical involvement in the life of others can teach you more than an education.

5. The disciples of Jesus Christ modeled their leadership style after His and became better leaders. Today we are supposed to do the same, if we have the desire to become better leaders.

---

23 Byrne and Bradley, *"Culture's Influence on Leadership Efficiency"*

Nightly Activity

The Nightly Activity is designed to track the productivity of your everyday life to analyze how the 31 day journey is helping you to become a better person and a better leader. It also serves as a journal. As you advance in your journey, you should look back every day and constantly check the nightly activity page to see whether you are improving. Circle a number you consider to be the overall productivity level of your day. Color the circle you consider to be your spiritual growth level today. See Appendix I.

I observed:_____

_____

I learned:_____

_____

I changed:_____

_____

Review of the day:_____

_____

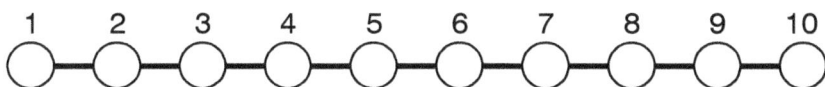

1   2   3   4   5   6   7   8   9   10

WALKING BY FAITH:
Motivation

Yesterday we talked about leadership style and how important it is to be a motivator. The more motivated the team members (followers) are, the more successful the ministry will be. It is also true in the case of the leader. Leaders need to be motivated every day, and for a Christian leader the best source of such motivation is the living Word of God.

Word of Encouragement

Jesus said, "I am the good shepherd. The good shepherd lays down his life for the sheep... The reason my Father loves me is that I lay down my life-only to take it up again. No one takes it from me, but I lay it down of my own accord. I have authority to lay it down and authority to take it up again. This command I received from my Father." (John 10:11,17-18)

We can take the example of a teacher. According to research, the two most important satisfiers in the motivation of teachers are achievement and recognition. A more participative style of management will allow for a greater degree of satisfaction in the areas of achievement and recognition, and for a much reduced degree of dissatisfaction with administration and with relationships between peers. Increased satisfaction with reduced dissatisfaction will result in improved teachers' motivation. It will bring an improved likelihood of success in the integration of faith and learning. The administration is generally concerned with day-today operations, committees, and centralized control, to the extent that innovative decision-making and concern for people as individuals who have something worthwhile to contribute is smothered by the demands of routine administrative tasks.

In his monograph, "Teacher Motivation: An Essential Requirement in the Integration of Faith and Learning in Seventh-Day Adventist Colleges," Allen F. Stembridge refers to the work of Barry Richman and Richard Farmer. He states, "Richman and Farmer…make a clear distinction between administration and management." He then quotes, "Administration implies more routine decision making and operation, and the implementation of goals, priorities, and strategies, usually determined by others…. It is also more concerned with internal monitoring and control…. To us, at least, administration implies bureaucracy.[24]" Administrators are the decision makers, and it is in their control to develop strategies and determine visions, goals, and certain operations to improve the quality of an organization; they are also more concerned with internal monitoring and control. If they are motivated to follow the biblical model of leadership, then they can lead others to follow their vision. For your followers, your motivation is the key to effectiveness in your ministry.

I have seen and heard a number of individuals who have taken motivation as their profession (they are called motivational speakers). One of the best examples of a motivational person is your gym instructor. There is a YMCA fitness center near my house. Last summer I decided to have a trainer for my gym exercise. The instructor did not give me a speech; actually, he was a very monotone guy. However, what he did was excellent. He challenged me to be more disciplined. I was paying per hour, so if he came and I was not there, I would still have to pay him. I am a very punctual person, so there was no way that I would miss even a second of the time he was on the clock. I also started

---

24 Stembridge, *"Teacher Motivation"*

coming half an hour earlier than he, so I could complete the warm up work before he got there. The second day when he saw me already sweaty and all warmed up, he had to show me some new exercises. The next day I came an hour early and finished my warm up and the other stretch exercises I knew he would ask me to do. When he arrived and asked me to follow the routine exercise from the day before, I told him I had already finished. He said, "You are getting more out of your money than I expected." I have learned to be a great motivator for myself. Other factors and people are just additional assistance to encourage you to continue motivating yourself.

This leads me to another counseling situation in which I was involved. I was counseling this young man who was always stressed and depressed. He hated his life, the world, and anyone who seemed a little happy. He always complained that God was not listening to him. He had been asking God to give him only one thing: Happiness. I spent hours with him on a daily basis. Every other day he came with a new issue, and I tried to walk him through the situation (that could have been worse). He said, "I just can't get along with people." I gave him the example of our friendship and stated that he and I had been getting along pretty well so far. Days continued passing and I was losing my patience; while this gentleman acknowledged that he had problems, he was not willing to work on his issues. (Although, according to him, he was.) I am sure he wanted instant results by coming to me and getting motivated to live another day on this earth. When I couldn't take it any longer, I told him, "No one else can help you unless you help yourself." God is gracious and wants to work on us, but if we will not allow it He will not do it.

Step 22 *towards becoming a better leader is to be a self-motivator. Use the Scriptures to become a self-motivator.*

Questions and Comments of Day 22

The following are a few key points that I consider very significant in terms of exemplary leadership and motivation:

1. What is the source of your motivation? Is it through listening to a sermon, reading a book, or simply praying? Whatever it is, make it a pattern of your life so that those whom you influence as a leader may see it as an example.

2. Christ spent hours and hours alone with His father praying. What does that teach you?

3. Our God in heaven wants us to come to Him for the encouragement to get through another day. All we need to do is simply obey him and change those behaviors He dislikes.

Nightly Activity

The Nightly Activity is designed to track the productivity of your everyday life to analyze how the 31 day journey is helping you to become a better person and a better leader. It also serves as a journal. As you advance in your journey, you should look back every day and constantly check the nightly activity page to see whether you are improving. Circle a number you consider to be the overall productivity level of your day. Color the circle you consider to be your spiritual growth level today. See Appendix I.

I observed:_____

_____

I learned:_____

_____

I changed:_____

_____

Review of the day:_____

_____

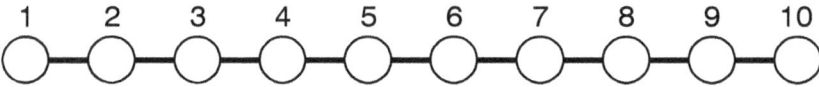

Day 23

WALKING BY FAITH:
Delegation and Empowerment

A dear Christian friend who is the director of a camp brought something to my attention which I thought very significant to remember as we are walking by faith. Many times we forget we are simply human beings and error is inevitable. Perfection belongs to God alone, and He does not expect us to be perfect; yet He wants us to strive for perfection, and as Christians we should be working toward perfection. One day when we are no longer slaves of this flesh we will

Word of Encouragement

According to Tucker, even the Christians' harshest critics acknowledged that the early church was sharing her faith with the poor and needy. One critic by the name Celsus writes, "Their aim is to convince only worthless and contemptible people, idiots, slaves, poor women, and children they behave like mountebanks and beggars; they would not dare to address an audience of intelligent men...but if they see a group of young people or slaves or rough folk, there they push themselves in and seek to win the admiration of the crowd. It is the same in private houses. We see wool- carders, cobblers, washermen, people of the utmost ignorance and lack of education.[25]*"*

25 Tucker, *Jerusalem to Irian Jaya*

be perfect, as He wants us to be. Until that day, we need to confess that we are not perfect. Therefore, as leaders we can't expect perfection from our followers.

A certain Christian leader has a staff of 90 people, but I saw him running everywhere, doing everything, and getting worn out. I just could not understand why a person would hire such a huge staff and pay their salaries when he is trying to accomplish everything by himself.

It is good to be careful and vigilant, but if you don't trust the decisions of your followers or the leadership you have appointed then you can't be a good leader. If you are a good leader then your followers will be good leaders too. And the best way to do that is through delegation and empowerment. Christ has called us to make disciples, and when you are making disciples you need to trust them and let them make choices. They will learn from their mistakes.

Delegation is a style of leadership where the leader trusts the decision-making ability of his/her followers. By delegation, the leaders allow the followers to make decisions on their behalf while the leaders remain responsible for the decisions that are made. A leader cannot do everything all the time, therefore the leader sets priorities, and delegates certain tasks. Nevertheless, one must remember that this only happens when employees or followers are able to analyze the situation and determine what needs to be done and how to do it. In the commercial world, empowerment is power or authority given to an agent to make decisions on behalf of the leader. Nanette Page and Cheryl E. Czuba introduce their understanding of the term empowerment. They see empowerment as a multi-dimensional social process, "...that helps people gain control over their own lives. It is a process that fosters power in people for use in their own lives, their communities and in their society, by acting on issues they define as important.[26]" A leader encourages followers to take part in decision making; he makes them part of the team. The World Bank suggests that empowerment is the process of "enhancing the capacity of individuals or groups to make choices and to transform those choices into desired actions and outcomes.[27]"

Delegation and empowerment both are very important in the biblical leadership style. For Christian leaders, it is essential to disciple and train followers. When the followers become team members and take 'ownership,' then they are obligated to repeat the process with their subordinates. Christ took twelve disciples and trained them, and when He was sure of their ability to make decisions, He sent them to do the same work on His behalf (Matt. 28:19-20). However, in such a leadership style, we need to be assured of divine help in decision-making.

When as a leader you empower your followers and delegate your work among them, you are giving them a sense of ownership. They can feel that they are a part of the big picture. Once I conducted a very small experiment during a leadership course. As soon as the students entered the class, I gave them the job to clean their hall before starting our class. About a half an hour passed, and the hall was not cleaned enough to start the class. Well, after a few weeks (when the hall got a little dirty), I divided them into three teams, and I appointed three leaders for them. Each team was given a task and the hall was done in five minutes! When you ask people to do work, everyone debates who will start. In the absence of a leader, the followers are like sheep wandering in the wilderness. But when I provided them with a leader, those leaders (who were just like their peers) felt ownership, as well as each group feeling that they had a direction. The leader empowered and delegated group work among individuals, so the work was done in no time.

---

26 Page and Czuba, *"Empowerment: What Is It?"*
27 World Bank, *A Guide to the World Bank, 2nd Edition*

If you are about to wear out because you do everything, please consider delegating your work. Trust in the Lord that your followers will do well, and pray for them! Remember the very first day, when you started the same work, and how you felt a sense of ownership.

> **Step 23** *towards becoming a better leader is to learn how to delegate your work among your followers, then to empower them to continue the good work.*

Questions and Comments of Day 23

1. If, over a long period of time, you have developed the pattern of doing everything by yourself, then it is very normal not to let control go into other's hands. Besides, being in control makes us feel better. If you are in the habit of it, God is the only one who can remove this stone from your path in order to shape you into a better leader.

2. It is just not right for a Christian leader to practice power and control. If you want to earn the trust of your followers, you must trust them first.

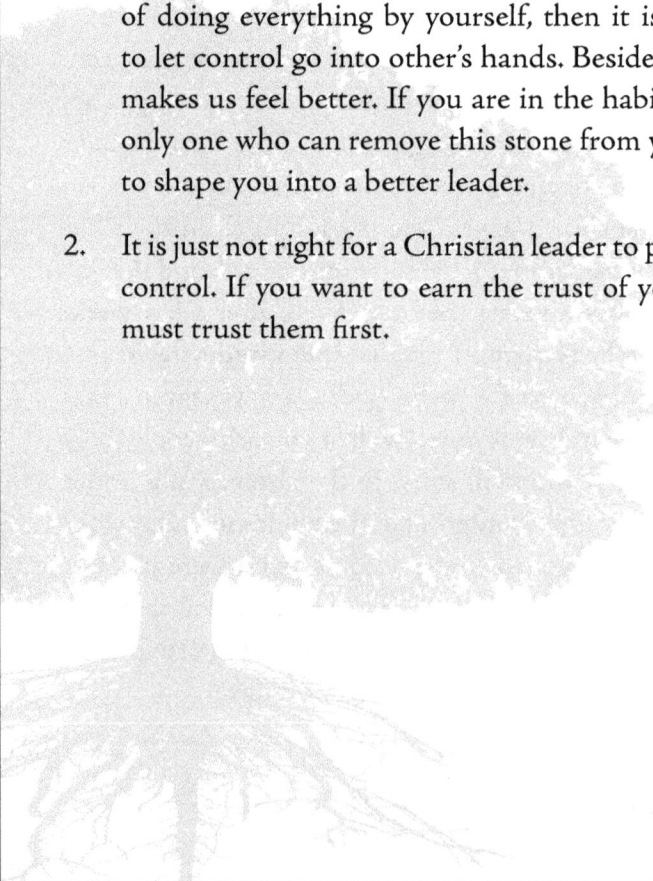

Nightly Activity

The Nightly Activity is designed to track the productivity of your everyday life to analyze how the 31 day journey is helping you to become a better person and a better leader. It also serves as a journal. As you advance in your journey, you should look back every day and constantly check the nightly activity page to see whether you are improving. Circle a number you consider to be the overall productivity level of your day. Color the circle you consider to be your spiritual growth level today. See Appendix I.

I observed:

I learned:

I changed:

Review of the day:

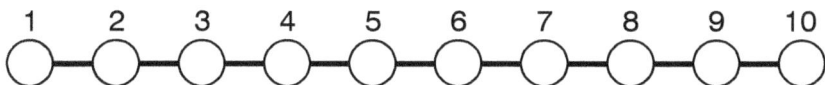

| 1 | 2 | 3 | 4 | 5 | 6 | 7 | 8 | 9 | 10 |

WALKING BY FAITH:
Vision and Communication

Dictionary.com defines vision as, "a vivid, imaginative conception or anticipation", for example, "visions of wealth and glory.[28]" If you pick up any book on leadership that is written in the last decade I bet you will find vision and mission to be a crucial part of leadership. It is very hard to define vision to its fullest extent, because when someone talks about vision, he or she is referring to the ability of someone to see the present through future eyes-to improve the present to make the future better. Vision is not daydreaming, but it is the ability of a leader to see into the future without being far-sighted, and to remain rooted in the present without being near-sighted. It is a tremendously powerful force to break through the lines of ordinary leadership into excellent leadership. A vision serves as a bull's eye at which a leader aims his/her energy and resources. It inspires a leader to keep moving despite the obstacles and constant resistance. These could be fear of failure, negative responses from superiors, peers, or employees, financial difficulty, or lack of resources.

You may find many people who have vision; they always have new ideas and goals, but they will not be good leaders if they do not know how to execute those ideas. It is important to be

---

28 Dictionary.com, "Vision"

visionary-but without strategy that vision is worth nothing. I would say that if a vision is worth a dollar, then a plan to execute is worth a million dollars! Vision does not start in the head like a dream; it originates in your heart.

John C. Maxwell provides three levels of leadership:

- You're in charge,
- You're Cool, and
- You make things happen.[29]

Now here is my question: what statement comes true in your life? Do you think people follow you because they want to, or because you are in charge, or because you are cool, or because you make things happen? In terms of fulfilling the vision, I suggest you should have all three. If God has put you in charge, you need to make sure that you are doing God's work and not abusing your power. Be gentle and kind to your followers.

Also make sure that being a Christian and having a meek spirit does not give the wrong idea to others so that they can slack off. God is an active God, and He loves when we put 100% of our effort into fulfilling the task entrusted to us. According to Scripture, we are supposed to be doing whatever we do wholeheartedly, for the glory of God.

Ruth Tucker writes about one of the early church missionaries who had a vision to reach out to the Goths, a barbarian tribe outside the Roman Empire (living in the area of present day Romania). "For forty years Ulfilas conducted evangelistic work among the Goths, a work that was highly successful, but one that was hampered by persecution.[30]" Ulfilas' vision was fulfilled in his efforts to provide the Goths with the Scriptures. The Goths' native tongue was an unwritten language, therefore Ulfilas devised an alphabet for the language and translated the Bible

---

29 Maxwell, *Developing the Leader Within You*
30 Tucker, *Jerusalem to Irian Jaya*

from the Greek, "without losing the Gothic idiom." Ulfilas died at the age of seventy during his mission to Constantinople—but his vision lived forever. When God calls, He gives us a vision to fulfill that call.

Vision alone cannot attain the desired results; it is dead without communicating the vision to others. When the vision of a leader becomes the vision of the whole organization, it changes the future of the organization. It is a force within a leader that spreads like wildfire when properly communicated to others. The key word is communication; if the vision is not being discussed and has not been invested in by the community, it remains a dream or just an idea.

A well communicated vision can serve as the glue that binds individuals in the group to achieve a common goal. Once the followers of a leader (either in a social, religious, political or company setting) understand their leader's vision, they can try to accomplish it.

Communication is not only verbalizing your thoughts and ideas, but it is a dynamic action. Communication can be done in various ways. We know from our previous discussions that the biblical concept of leadership is servanthood. Christian leaders are not to mistreat their followers, but to respect them as brothers and sisters in Christ. Christ was the perfect model of leadership when He was on earth through His acts of service. It is essential for leaders to understand their spiritual gifts in order to measure their leadership style as Christian leaders. The goal of understanding spiritual gifts is to discover one's place of service in the body of Christ. You may match your gifts with a place of service that already exists in your local church or ministry (such as a need for a Bible teacher, counselor, youth leader, elder, deacon or even a pastor). Or you may match your gifts with a ministry that exists outside your local church. Your gifts may also motivate you to find places of ministry that do not yet exist in your church, i.e., if the church needs an outreach coordinator, worship arts pastor or drama director to encourage more people, God may use your gifts to start such a ministry. The bottom line is that God gifted you to serve His body. The adventure is discovering both the gift and place of service, for the good of all (1 Cor. 12:7). The question is this: what are your personal perceptions of your giftedness, and what have others in the body said about how you serve the church?

Once you have discovered your spiritual gifts, you need to communicate them to others. People need to be aware of your giftedness. Either you can communicate them though your actions or you need to speak up. No one will know that you have certain gifts unless they see the execution. If you are a member of a church and you believe that you have the gift to lead or direct a Sunday school, then you need to let the leadership know. If you attend a church and a small group faithfully, others might get an idea that you could be a potential leader-but still you have to demonstrate those gifts by serving in the body of Christ.

Communication is essential for a leader; when a leader doesn't know how to communicate, the consequences are not limited to the leader, but include everyone who follows the leader. In my experience counseling couples I have found the most devastating element of conflict and fights is lack of communication. It is very hard when you do not communicate, yet expect other people to understand. If you say your wants and opinions directly, it reduces the stress on both ends. You cannot expect your followers to know your mind. Is it possible? Yes, in some cases when you have spent many years with your followers it is possible for them to know your mind. Some people may understand you on a personal basis or know your daily routines, and nothing more. But most of us are constantly changing as we grow in our faith and as we age. With those changes come new ways of dealing with things, and of doing things differently. If you fail to communicate to your followers, I am sorry. It is not their fault if they are confused.

> **Step 24** *towards becoming a better leader is to learn how to communicate your vision and beliefs.*

Questions and Comments of Day 24

1. Do you know if you have a vision yet? Take your time and pray, and ask God to open your eyes that you may find your purpose in this life. Your vision for yourself is one of the most important things as a leader.

2. If you think your vision has not been picked up by others after years of training, sessions and table meetings, probably you have not communicated your vision to your followers-in their language. I am not talking about the language barrier, but about the level of their intellectual understanding, cultural understanding, and spiritual understanding.

3. Jesus communicated His vision and message to every person with whom He came in contact, to his/her level of understanding. He spoke in parables to the common man, and addressed the hypocrisy of religious leaders of His time with boldness.

4. If you have already communicated your vision (and your followers have understood it on every level), but now your vision is falling apart because your followers are not doing what they are supposed to do, maybe it is time to rethink your vision. It is possible that they are doing exactly the same

thing they were supposed to, but maybe your expectations have changed because circumstances have changed. Many organizations (especially ministries) look at their vision quite often, and they make modifications or changes if they are needed. So don't hesitate in communicating your vision.

Nightly Activity

The Nightly Activity is designed to track the productivity of your everyday life to analyze how the 31 day journey is helping you to become a better person and a better leader. It also serves as a journal. As you advance in your journey, you should look back every day and constantly check the nightly activity page to see whether you are improving. Circle a number you consider to be the overall productivity level of your day. Color the circle you consider to be your spiritual growth level today. See Appendix I.

I observed:_____

_____

I learned:_____

_____

I changed:_____

_____

Review of the day:_____

_____

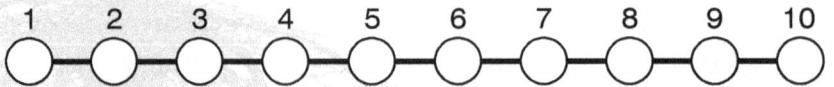

WALKING BY FAITH:
Integrity

In Christianity, we find the word "integrity" to be a trade-mark of Christian life. If you think you have hidden something or have not told the full truth to others, then it means you are not a man or woman of integrity. Doing the right thing, whether someone is watching you or not, whether you are under persecution or not (without thinking about the consequences), is integrity. I was teaching a class to young Christian men and women, and at some point I mentioned that I have never had drugs or alcohol. All the students were astonished. They could not believe that in my whole life I had not tried anything. Well, in America, when you enter in public high school or go to college, it is almost inevitable that at one time or another you will get hooked up with drugs. By the grace of God, I

Word of Encouragement

"For by Him all things were created both in the heavens and on earth, visible and invisible, whether thrones or dominions or rulers or authorities-all things have been created by Him and for Him. And He is before all things and in Him all things hold together. He is also head of the body, the church, and He is the beginning, the first-born from the dead; so that He Himself might come to have first place in everything. For it was the Father's good pleasure for all the fullness to dwell in Him."
(Colossians 1:16-18)

---

was not interested in those things, and God kept me clean. But this group shouted out, "Don't be modest!" One of the young women even said to me, "Most of the preachers and teachers lie when it comes to these kinds of things." But I was not lying or hiding: I was simply stating the truth. Sometimes it hurts when you tell the truth and no one believes you, because they don't want to hear the truth.

We should do the right thing no matter what the circumstances or consequences, whether someone is watching or not. Also, you need to do what you say or suggest that others do. Jesus was against the Jewish religious leaders because they were hypocrites. They demanded that others follow the law and do every right thing, but they themselves were far away from God. In Matthew 23:27 Jesus called them "whitewashed tombs" because they appeared very clean on the outside but inside were filled with filthiness and garbage. Our prime example, Jesus Christ, did what he said. I liked a question I read in a book, and I ask it every time I talk about integrity. "If you weren't you, would you follow you?" If your answer is a deep pause or no, then you need to work on becoming a leader of integrity. The Scriptures tell us, "Show yourself in all respects to be a model of good works, and in your teaching show integrity, and dignity" (Tit 2:7 ESV).

One of the places where integrity is compromised the most is where everyone is doing something and you are not. This "everyone" could be a local community, society, or even a church congregation; it could also be your peer group or friends. The greatest test of integrity comes when you are pressured by circumstances to partake of something you consider wrong. I have a very close friend who does not drink, and who loves the Lord and promised God that she would not drink. One day during summer break she decided to visit her parents. Her friends came to visit her at her parents' home and they brought some alcohol with them. Her sisters and the rest of the family drank; when she saw everyone drinking she didn't want to be the odd one out, so she decided to compromise her integrity. If you are not doing something at one place but doing the same thing in other places (regardless of whether people judge you or not), you are not being true to yourself. Exodus 23:2 says, "You must not do wrong just because everyone else is doing it" (NCV).

I have learned discipline through being true to myself. I decided to give up unhealthy food. In America it is hard to find healthy food, and all the healthy food is super-expensive. I gave up sugar, cheese, red meat, soda, and a few other things. One day late at night I was passing by my fridge and looked into it. I found fresh cookies, and I wanted to have a bite. I thought it wouldn't hurt if I took a tiny bite, so I took a very tiny bite. All of a sudden, my conscience started shouting aloud that I should not be eating, because by eating (even a tiny bit) I will be going against own principle of disciplining myself. How would I face someone who knows that I don't eat sugar anymore? So I just spit it out. Thank God, I am not a diabetic! But I promised myself that I would not use sugar.

Sometimes minor things which do not hurt others find a place in our hearts to go against our integrity. It's like Paul says, "For the desires of the flesh are against the Spirit, and the desires of the Spirit are against the flesh, for these are opposed to each other, to keep you from doing the things you want to do" (Gal 5:17 ESV).

Step 25 towards becoming a better leader is to become a man or a woman of integrity first.

Questions and Comments of Day 25

1. If you know that the person you are looking at in the mirror is worthy to follow, you have already succeeded to the level of a good leader.

2.   When was the last time you felt the need to go around the truth in expressing what you believe? If you do not say 'yes' for yes and 'no' for no, you may be facing a giant enemy and that enemy is you.

3.   Your integrity defines you, whether or not you are a good person and worthy of leadership.

4.   Do you do the right thing because you want to please people, or do you do the right thing because that is what your integrity demands you to do?

5.   Do your family members consider you a person of integrity? Can they testify without a doubt?

Nightly Activity

The Nightly Activity is designed to track the productivity of your everyday life to analyze how the 31 day journey is helping you to become a better person and a better leader. It also serves as a journal. As you advance in your journey, you should look back every day and constantly check the nightly activity page to see whether you are improving. Circle a number you consider to be the overall productivity level of your day. Color the circle you consider to be your spiritual growth level today. See Appendix I.

I observed:_____

_____

I learned:_____

_____

I changed:_____

_____

Review of the day:_____

_____

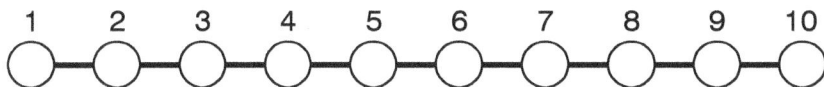

Day 26

WALKING BY FAITH:
Lone Ranger or Team Player

One pleasant evening in late summer 1998, a man showed up at my parents' house. He rode an old fashioned bicycle, which looked as old as he was. Its rusty frame, poor quality tires, and absence of brakes made me think it belonged to his father, or even his grandfather. As he stepped from his bike, I could see sweat oozing from his body-forming drops like rain as it touched the dusty narrow path. He removed from his back a battered black leather bag, with the corners crudely patched with white thread and the zipper replaced with nylon string. It looked more like a sack that people use for groceries or laundry than a backpack. He respectfully introduced himself while digging into the pack and removing a low quality, one color newspaper leaflet with a black and white image of himself marked in the center of the text. He handed me the flyer with this explanation: "Sir, I am running for one of the district seats in town and I'm asking for your vote."

The candidate was very courageous in what he was doing, very inspiring and, perhaps on some level, unique. However, productivity was zero.

Word of Encouragement

Jesus said, "Salt is good; but if the salt becomes unsalty, with what will you make it salty again? Have salt in yourselves, and be at peace with one another." (Mark 9:50)

If a man doesn't have a following before running for government office, how can he influence others to keep the system running smoothly, even if he somehow wins the campaign and secures a seat? This man, to me, represented one in desperate need of an understanding of what leadership is all about. If you are walking down a street and thinking you are leading others, but when you look back and find no one following, then it's time to confront the reality that you are not yet a leader. But if you initiate something and others follow, then, my friend, you are a leader.

The good news is that leadership can be learned. If you say you are a leader but people don't acknowledge your leadership, then you are mistaken. Here is another scenario. In a group (either large or small), you find people following you who respect your leadership, yet you realize you are doing everything yourself. Either others do not volunteer, or you're reluctant to delegate responsibility. The rule of leadership says you are not yet an effective leader. If you are trying to accomplish everything in a self-motivated ministry, I would say, my friend, "Me, Myself and I," do not qualify as followers. Rather than a leader, you are a Lone Ranger.

Jesus gave us a very valuable example of an exemplary and effective leader. When He began His public ministry, the Scripture tells us that the first thing He did was to call His twelve disciples who followed Him throughout His earthly ministry. When He sent them out for ministry, He paired them off in twos. There is wisdom in this. "For if they fall, one will lift up his fellow. But woe to him who is alone when he falls and has not another to lift him up!" (Eccl. 4:10 ESV).

The Lone Ranger is not a biblical concept and every Christian should avoid being one. However, there are some exceptions to working alone; i.e, when there are no other believers, or no one who understands leadership, or until others are trained. But these situations do not endorse the Lone Ranger concept. Your first order should be to develop teamwork. Not only will a team enable you to accomplish more, but also we can encourage each other in times of trouble and discouragement. Married people often find that their spouses can be the best companions they could wish for.

One of the best ways to form a team is through communicating your vision with those who share the same desires with you. When I moved to New York City, I did not know anyone and I had no clue as to what, where, when, or how to start. I only knew that I had a vision to reach Muslim people in New York City. I communicated this vision to everyone I met and, in time, God gave me a team to work with. A team that shares the same vision can be a precious treasure.

The Lone Ranger concept leads us to the next step along our journey of building a team. When I took my job in New York City, the very first thing I asked God to do was to help me build a team. A team does not necessarily mean twenty, thirty or more people. It simply means that someone other than yourself shares your vision and is willing to assist in completing it. This can be a tough task at times. A general rule of thumb is to bring God in the midst of everything, and ask for His help. I am absolutely certain that without His direction, all my knowledge and efforts would come to nothing.

In team-building, it is crucial to include those who are not like-minded, as well as those who are. This allows for different opinions and viewpoints, which are essential for positive growth. It is not a good thing to have everyone agree with you every time. You either run into an unresolved problem, or it means you are producing clones of yourself. It's like hanging out with your sports equipment (or cooking utensils) and doing your own thing-with no disagreement or input from anyone. However, disagreement in everything is not healthy either. So an appropriate balance of both would make a strong, productive, and healthy team.

The key point in team building is not to look at the differences of opinion, but what each member of the team thinks about the vision and how they contribute to it. Do they see the vision with the same eye? If they have disagreements on the vision you have cast, then probably the team you are working with is worse than being a Lone Ranger. For example, Harvard University originally was established for one purpose to train pastors and missionaries. Today, it is no longer a Christian institution. Somehow the vision of the founding team was replaced by a later team. And when, finally, the majority agreed with the disagreement of the minority, Harvard became a secular school. It happens to all sorts of organizations, but if you disciple and train others, they will be ready to take your place when you retire or go to your eternal rest.

Nehemiah is a fantastic example of a leader who considered team-building the first step toward accomplishing the vision. When he heard about the sad condition of Jerusalem, a vision was born. He envisioned how he would bring that vision to reality. When he arrived in Jerusalem he built a team, delegated the work, and focused on the vision. The team he gathered was one in attaining the vision.

Team-building may take some time, but once you have a team other tasks will become much easier. I like the mission of Campus Crusade for Christ. They emphasize team building; from small projects to major ones, their ministry depends on team-building. One of my friends and his wife are raising their support to go to Africa as missionaries. The very first thing they were asked to do was to build a team of those who would support them both financially and spiritually, and who would accompany them on short mission trips. They are also building a team in this particular African country where they will serve for the rest of their lives. My friend is leading short-term mission teams on a consistent basis, which is also part of team-building. These people will be their resource when they move to Africa.

Step 26 towards becoming a better leader is to build a team that shares your vision. If you look back and find that no one is following, you are in the race alone. Don't be a Lone Ranger.

Questions and Comments of Day 26

1. You may have been doing everything without a team; probably you want to build a team, but do not know how. You can start with sharing your vision. Let people know what you want to accomplish.

2. If you are running aimlessly or failing to communicate your vision with others, you have neither fellow or follower.

3. If you are habitually doing the job of ten people and are proud of it, please pause and rethink: Is this the best way to serve God?

4. If you have been communicating your vision with others for many years yet have no one to join your team, then I suggest that you first pray. Secondly, rethink your vision. It's better to wait than to be a Lone Ranger.

5. I understand it is easy to hire people to be part of a team, but their qualifications and experience are no guarantee that they would help you to fulfill your vision. If people want to join your team because they want to contribute to your vision, then you are already on your way to becoming a better leader.

6. Are you hired to fulfill a vision or to cast the vision? Either way, you need a team that understands your desires about the vision.

7. If, after years of efforts you still don't have people who want to join you, you may have to change your leadership style in order to have a team.

8. Your influence serves as an attraction to bring people into the team.

Nightly Activity

The Nightly Activity is designed to track the productivity of your everyday life to analyze how the 31 day journey is helping you to become a better person and a better leader. It also serves as a journal. As you advance in your journey, you should look back every day and constantly check the nightly activity page to see whether you are improving. Circle a number you consider to be the overall productivity level of your day. Color the circle you consider to be your spiritual growth level today. See Appendix I.

I observed:_____

_____

I learned:_____

_____

I changed:_____

_____

Review of the day:_____

_____

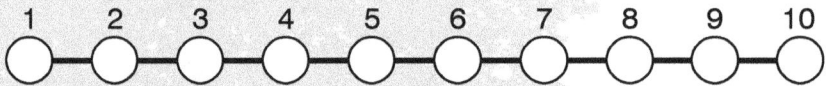

| 1 | 2 | 3 | 4 | 5 | 6 | 7 | 8 | 9 | 10 |

WALKING BY FAITH:
Obstacles

While living in a third world country, I could not imagine that life would be so complicated in America, the most powerful country on the face of the earth. I was hired as a youth pastor to start a youth ministry at a church in Philadelphia, PA. Many of the elders were interested in targeting a nearby community college, but the senior pastor was more concerned about a couple of high school students in the church. I decided to start my work at the grassroots. When there is not much of a structure in place and complications are discouraging you, it is better to start from scratch. The first thing I wanted to do was shape a vision and a mission statement before I implemented any technique to bring youth into the church.

Immediately I ran into piles of obstacles. Some very loving and kind folks deliberately opposed the changes I was making. The church was not doing too well financially, and every member was important. Now, when you run into an obstacle,

Word of Encouragement

"But now you also, put them all aside: anger, wrath, malice, slander, and abusive speech from your mouth. Do not lie to one another, since you laid aside the old self with its evil practices and have put on the new self who is being renewed to a true knowledge according to the image of the One who created him."
(Colossians 3:8-10)

what do you do? Do you pass it by, change your path, break or move the obstacle out of your way, or simply ignore the obstacle? Most of us at one time or another have done all of the above; if you have missed one or two, let me assure you that you will have your share.

As a leader, your job is not to avoid obstacles but to remove them carefully that they may not hurt your followers. But how would you do that without hurting someone? It is like a picture I once saw on the internet. The guy in the picture had a big, round, metal rod pierced through his side. Would it be possible to remove such a big object without hurting the patient? Realistically speaking, no. I'm sure the pain would remain long after the rod was removed. The same rule applies to obstacles in your ministry. Either the obstacle is a tangible or an intangible thing. Tangible things can be compared to unrepaired buildings, no building to begin with, or members with a rebellious nature. It also includes health problems (of your own, or of loved ones), lack of adequate finances, or unemployment. Intangibles are recognized in relationships; evidenced by emotion, love, fear, likes and dislikes, faith, honesty, disagreement, and dishonesty, integrity, et cetera.

When you deal with people in a ministry to remove obstacles, you can never be too careful. You are going to hurt someone at some level. The human mind says less hurt is better than more, but leadership requires extraordinary stability in maintaining the equilibrium. In other words, if less hurt makes things shaky, a little less complicated, and temporarily stable, it is essential to let the greater hurt come in order to remove the obstacle for good. It is like the bandage on a wound; it is more painful if you are ripping it off slowly because of the fear of pain. Pain plus the fear of pain makes it ten times worse than the actual pain. It is better to rip it off at once and avoid the torture of fear.

That is exactly that what I did at that church. I knew I would not keep everyone happy, so I did what I believed God wanted me to do. After determining the vision and mission statement, I looked at the logistical parts of the youth ministry. Many other factors entered into the story, but the end result was that I brought about quite a rivalry against me. People are not eager recipients of quick change. I learned that you can't make changes on your own watch; wait for the right time. Go with others the extra mile, wait and observe, and never tire of waiting, even when you know that you have been waiting too long. There is wisdom in waiting and foolishness in haste. In fact, we who trust in the Lord are commanded to wait. The Scriptures are full of such references. Psalm 27:14 says, "Wait for the LORD; be strong, and let your heart take courage; wait for the LORD!" (ESV).

When you are removing a major obstacle, you need to remember that it is going to require extraordinary patience and waiting. I have asked too many times, "when is the wait too long?" I believe, if we surrender ourselves to God's will, then there is nothing to worry about. Wait, wait, and wait. If you are like me then you know how hard it is to wait, especially when the obstacle is major and needs immediate attention. It is difficult when your mind says you can do it, but your heart tells you, "Believe what the Scripture says." One of the problems visionary leaders face is that they won't wait.

> *Step 27 towards becoming a better leader is to acknowledge that waiting is the key element in the process of leading others. When you depend on God and wait, He comes to the rescue and removes the obstacle for you Himself.*

Questions and Comments of the Day 27

1. Moses was a wonderful leader, but His lack of patience kept him from entering the promised land. He should have known from previous experiences that the nation he was leading whined all the time, and that every obstacle so far had been removed by God. I wonder if he had waited for God's command before he hit the rock if God might not have given him the same command anyway.

2. Do you view an obstacle as a stressful situation or as an opportunity? Do you perceive the idea of failure as a learning experience? The idea of failure as a learning experience is the core tenet of looking at stress positively. Psychologically speaking we don't like failure, and we don't like putting time and effort into something just to see it unfulfilled. It can be incredibly demoralizing. So this idea of seeing a new, risky endeavor as an opportunity to learn is a way to mitigate this feeling. When you don't look at a failure as the end but rather as the beginning of something new, it is easy to handle any stress. Tomorrow we will look at this in detail.

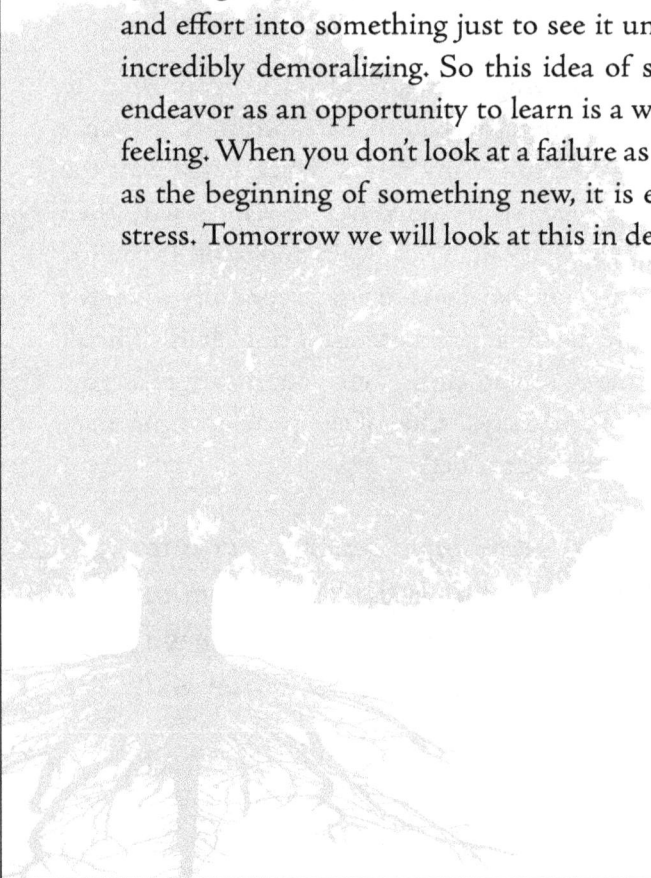

Nightly Activity

The Nightly Activity is designed to track the productivity of your everyday life to analyze how the 31 day journey is helping you to become a better person and a better leader. It also serves as a journal. As you advance in your journey, you should look back every day and constantly check the nightly activity page to see whether you are improving. Circle a number you consider to be the overall productivity level of your day. Color the circle you consider to be your spiritual growth level today. See Appendix I.

I observed:_____

_____

I learned:_____

_____

I changed:_____

_____

Review of the day:_____

_____

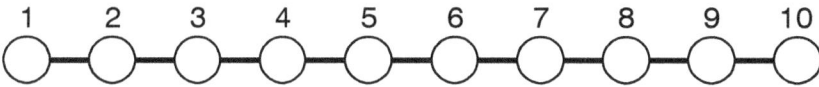

WALKING BY FAITH:
Conflict Resolution

onflict happens everywhere. Either you have experienced that as a leader, or you have not yet had to deal with conflict. A basic example is your brothers and sisters. Tell me if you have never had conflict with your siblings: how about classmates, parents or other family members? It happens regardless of age, gender, nationality, or social status. No one is immune to conflict. Whether you are a part of the conflict or simply a spectator, perpetrator or victim, invited or uninvited, you must learn how to resolve a conflict. If you are a Christian, then you may expect that every unsaved person (and many saved people) will be in conflict with you. It seems almost no one can avoid minor or major arguments, weak or strong disagreements. Some issue or problem will potentially drag you into a conflict zone, and if you don't know how to resolve it, I am sorry to say, you may cause damage to yourself or the other person (or both).

Many Christians think being a Christian means that you are under the God's protection, so nothing can harm you. Since you live in an imperfect world, you can't expect perfection. In a perfect world you would get along with everybody and anybody, but in reality, life demands us to be ready for everything, and anything you may consider bad. It's like health insurance. I consider the best health insurance to be the one which I never have to use. Thus it is imperative to be skilled in the area of conflict leadership, but our prayer should be that we may never have to use those skills.

On my first day of teaching a leadership class, I asked my students: "If you were me and running this five week program, what rules and regulations would you want enforced?" All the students suggested different rules and

regulations. Then I asked which ones should be zero tolerance. One of the students said, "Fighting with other classmates." It was not the answer I was looking for, but it did give me the opportunity to share about the importance of the leader's conflict resolution skills. I told them that they might get to the point of fighting if I, as a leader, could not resolve their conflicts. Some leaders prefer a temporary fix, just like a tiny patch on a busted water line (which potentially opens up again when the pressure builds up). A good leader resolves the conflict once and for all.

If you are the conflict resolver, make sure you are not becoming a part of the conflict. Keep yourself neutral, so both parties trust you and are willing to listen to you. But if you are one of the teams involved in the conflict, you may want to focus on complaints and issues, without bringing the debate down to who is right and who is wrong. A few years ago I worked with an Egyptian Coptic Christian. If you have an Egyptian friend you will understand what I am about to share, and if you know a Coptic Christian from Egypt then you will feel my frustration as a conflict resolver. This gentleman had a conflict with almost every female worker at the job, because he considered his opinion to be superior to those of women. One of these women filed a verbal complaint against him, saying that he was harassing her. So he came to me to ask for advice. I was one of the leaders at this place, so I told him I would talk to the big boss and take care of the problem. I assured him that I trusted him, and knew his actions were unintentional. Furthermore, I suggested that he 'let it go, don't be discouraged,' and certainly not to try to collect evidence to prove himself innocent because he was innocent.

I spoke to my boss and the matter was closed. However, this brother didn't let it go; he put his whole energy into proving himself innocent, taking away his passion for his job and his focus. People began seeing him as a distraction and an unethical worker. Other conflicts arose. He returned to me for advice. "Brother," I told him, "You need to let it go. You are innocent and no one has a problem. Put your heart in your work." The original issue did not put him in any trouble, but his focus on the issue made him a problem. When you become part of the problem, then it is hard to resolve it without consequences.

When the damage is done, you can't do anything other than learn from it and let it go. If you hold on to it, it's just a matter of time before it will eat you up. Your single conflict with an individual can expose you to a series of conflicts with many others. You need to look at the conflict which is already there. Ask yourself, is it worth fighting for? What is more important: winning a meaningless argument, or avoiding a conflict by letting the other person win? Sometimes when we lose we actually win, and sometimes even when we win-it does not feel like winning. Conflict resolution is a gift for those who are humble, patient, meek, and of a gentle spirit.

Conflict can be taken by leaders as an opportunity to grow:

- If leaders are committed to people in their organizations.

- If leaders feel a sense of control over the things that happen in their lives and in the lives of their followers.

- If leaders accept conflict and change as more of a challenge than as a threat.[31]

---

31 Kouzes and Posner, *The Leadership Challenge*

People who thrive under challenges consider it natural for things to change and anticipate the changes as useful stimuli for development. They see life as strenuous but exciting. In contrast, people who feel threatened think it is natural for things to remain stable, and they fear the possibility of change because it seems to disrupt comfort and security.

Control   **Commitment**

Leader

Challenge

Step 28 towards becoming a better leader is to learn how to resolve conflict, without becoming a part of the conflict.

Questions and Comments of Day 28

1. If you avoid conflict because you feel like you do not have enough knowledge or skills to resolve it, that avoidance could help you one or two times, but in the long run escape will never be the solution.

2. How do you resolve conflict? Do you bring both parties together to let them talk through their issues while you deal with them on a one-on-one basis? Personally, I prefer not to get involved in conflict resolution, unless the issue is brought to me by either party. If it is just a gossip report from a third party, I would rather excuse the person in a gentle spirit.

Nightly Activity

The Nightly Activity is designed to track the productivity of your everyday life to analyze how the 31 day journey is helping you to become a better person and a better leader. It also serves as a journal. As you advance in your journey, you should look back every day and constantly check the nightly activity page to see whether you are improving. Circle a number you consider to be the overall productivity level of your day. Color the circle you consider to be your spiritual growth level today. See Appendix I.

I observed:_____

_____

I learned:_____

_____

I changed:_____

_____

Review of the day:_____

_____

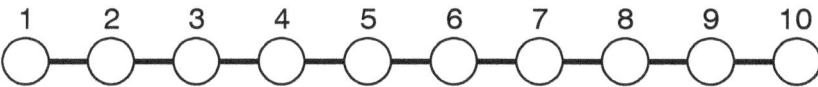

| 1 | 2 | 3 | 4 | 5 | 6 | 7 | 8 | 9 | 10 |

WALKING BY FAITH:
Strategy and Plans

Suppose you are an architect. You are given a vision and the promise of whatever money is needed, so long as you work out a strategy to fulfill that vision. What would you do? Would you walk away, come up with an unrealistic plan, or give something less than satisfactory? I assume you would give your best, to prove that you are the best in your field of expertise. It is similar when you are walking by faith, and you have to come up with a strategy and plan to launch a campaign, a new ministry, or just a part of a ministry. Although you are not promised any x, y, or z amount of money, you are promised a far greater reward- that of eternal life. If you put 20% effort in, you'll get 20% out; but if you put in 100% and ask the Lord to bless it, you will be blessed and the productivity of your work will be 100%. You can go to a business and management school to learn how to improve your strategy and planning, but it's your effort and desire that will make the difference.

Don't be afraid of mistakes, for mistakes teach us how to be better next time. At the end of a leadership program, I asked the students what type of leadership position they would like to have "President of the United States, or prince of Narnia," They thought I was joking. I went on. "Imagine you have been given your desired position. The next step is to determine what you would like to accomplish with your position." Excitement rippled through the room as they verbalized short and long term goals.

They were unaware of the fact that I was asking them to tell me about their visions. Once they found their visions, I asked them to come up with

a plan and strategy. This was the hardest part. Suddenly there was dead silence in the room. One student spoke up, "I thought you were just kidding." I took the opportunity to tell them that it is not too difficult to think about what you want to be and what you want to do, but it is hard for most of us to come up with a plan and strategy for how to accomplish that.

You can dream all day long, but without a plan and a strategy, it is just a dream. One of the best examples in terms of strategy and planning is Nehemiah. Nehemiah was concerned about his people, so he asked a few men who had returned from Judah: "And I asked them concerning the Jews who escaped, who had survived the exile, and concerning Jerusalem" (Neh. 1:2 ESV). When he heard about the desolation of Jerusalem, a vision was born. But before he communicated the vision, he went into the presence of God, and prayed. He confessed and repented on behalf of the Jewish nation, and reminded God of His promises and requested help. When he went before the king, the king asked him what troubled him. "So I prayed to the God of heaven. And I said to the king, 'If it pleases the king, and if your servant has found favor in your sight, that you send me to Judah, to the city of my fathers' graves, that I may rebuild it'" (Neh. 2:4-5 ESV). When the king had heard this request, he asked Nehemiah what he could do for him.

Nehemiah not only presented the vision, but also the strategy and plan for rebuilding the broken wall. He asked for letters for the governors, "the province beyond the river, that they may let me pass through until Judah" (Neh. 2:7 ESV), as well as letters for the keepers of king's forests that he might have the wood to build the wall. When we bring our empty hearts before God, to fill with His purpose, He blesses us with a vision. With that vision, He gives us the directions to reach that vision. Proverbs 3:5 says, "Trust in the LORD with all your heart, and do not lean on your own understanding."

Another positive attribute of Nehemiah's leadership was that he went to the original site and observed for himself. He did not rely on the reports he had heard, and probably reevaluated his strategy and plan to build the wall based on what he observed and saw. Many times when our plan is based on assumption, it needs to be different when it actually happens. The camp I go to every summer started renovating two cabins, with an expected budget of $50,000. Before completion, the work stopped because the estimate was wrong and they ran out of money. When the cabins were finally finished, the total expense was $95,000.

Sometimes we rush into implementing ideas and plans we think might work, and do not spend enough time in God's presence. When you walk by faith, you learn how to trust the Lord for every decision. Your strategy and plan are the blood and spirit of your vision. If you want to see your vision come true, you had better start asking God to give you a strategy and a plan to pull all the necessary tools and resources together to fulfill the vision.

According to one research study, "The ordinary executives who convinced others to join them on pioneering journeys followed the path of a three-phase strategy."[32]

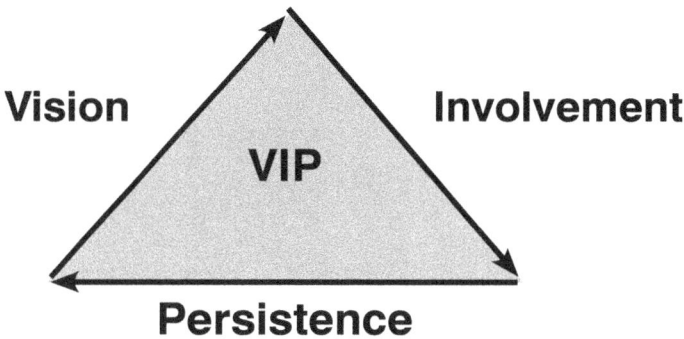

Vision   Involvement

VIP

Persistence

---

32 Kouzes and Posner, *The Leadership Challenge*

Vision: The leaders who were interviewed in the research by Kouzes and Posner had absolute and total personal belief in their abilities to make extraordinary things happen. However, I would say to place your absolute belief in Jesus and know that through Him you can do impossible things.

Involvement: You must be a part of the vision. Good leaders like Nehemiah not only lead but they participate in the progress of the work.

Persistence: We have already studied the importance of persistence. It means to never give up. It means relentless effort, steadfastness, competence, planning, attention to detail, and encouragement.

Step 29 towards becoming a better leader is to have a strategy and plan to fulfill the vision.

Questions and Comments of Day 29

1. If your strategy or plan is not working, you may want to revaluate it. It is okay to make mistakes. Just be persistent and ask God for His guidance.

2. If you are good with managing people but strategizing and planning trouble you, you may want to look at your spiritual and natural gifts to see if it is the right position for you to have now. We all are parts of the same body and all the parts of the body are equally important; you may fit in the ministry as another part.

Nightly Activity

The Nightly Activity is designed to track the productivity of your everyday life to analyze how the 31 day journey is helping you to become a better person and a better leader. It also serves as a journal. As you advance in your journey, you should look back every day and constantly check the nightly activity page to see whether you are improving. Circle a number you consider to be the overall productivity level of your day. Color the circle you consider to be your spiritual growth level today. See Appendix I.

I observed:_____

_____

I learned:_____

_____

I changed:_____

_____

Review of the day:_____

_____

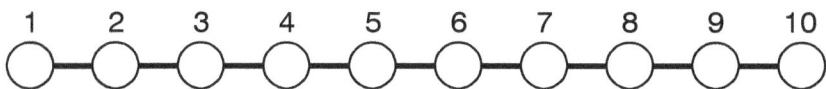

| 1 | 2 | 3 | 4 | 5 | 6 | 7 | 8 | 9 | 10 |

Day 30

WALKING BY FAITH:
Evaluation

I mentioned previously that I teach at a Bible school. After each course, I provide my students with an evaluation form. This evaluation form is primarily for the administration to see the student's response to the course, as well as finding ways to improve the course. I take these responses very seriously. I do not expect to be perfect in everything I do, nor do I expect my students to understand fully what I teach. My teaching comes from years of academia and practical experience, so how can I expect them to grasp it all in that brief period of time.

Recently I taught a Bible course, and began with this introduction: "I hope you get the most possible from this course, but if you do not take anything else, by the end of the course I expect you to be good observers."

Too often we fail to observe things around us, especially when it comes to compassion ministry. If we see someone in need, our first instinct is that the person needs to hear the word of God-he needs to know Jesus personally. I assure you that many of you think the same as I until the day when Christ spoke to me and I

Word of Encouragement

"Fight the good fight of faith; take hold of the eternal life to which you were called, and you made the good confession in the presence of many witnesses." (1 Timothy 6:12)

finally understood why He fed, then healed, and then preached. When it comes to compassion ministry, the one passage I like most is where James writes, "And one of you says to them, 'Go in peace, be warmed and filled,' without giving them the things needed for the body, what good is that?"(James 2:16)

The extreme of the same situation is when people are so concerned about meeting physical needs that they forget to talk about the ultimate Healer, our Jehovah Jirah, and Jesus Christ, the Savior of our souls. I remember a young man who shared about his recent conversion. He said, "I was drinking alcohol, using drugs, and was about to commit suicide," when he was taken to a psychologist and professional counselors. They put him on medication, gave him different exercises, and they charged a lot of money. "The reason why nothing was working was because they [the doctors and therapists] were treating my physical body when the problem resided in my soul, and no one was helping me fix my soul," he concluded.

I have seen numbers of ministries in the United States and abroad which are very good at meeting the physical needs of people, but when it comes to spiritual needs, they don't put much emphasis on Christ. When you evaluate your spiritual walk, when you evaluate the productivity of your ministry, and when you evaluate your personal relationship with God and His people, the first thing you should do is to observe. Evaluation cannot be done without good observation. Whether you are evaluating yourself or others are, someone is evaluating you; observation is the most significant step in the process. The accuracy of your observation in any field will prove your assumptions right or wrong; depending on the outcome, you can accurately evaluate your work.

In Christ we have grace, and this grace comes with responsibility, particularly if you are a teacher or a leader. The Scriptures advises, "Not many of you should become teachers, my brothers, for you know that we who teach will be judged with greater strictness" (James 3:1 ESV). The same rule applies to leaders. When God calls us to be leaders He does not evaluate us on the basis of human standards. His divine intentions are to use us for His glory and majesty, which is by faith in Jesus Christ, through the undeserving grace of God. Rom 12:6 says, "Having gifts that differ according to the grace given to us...," and Paul explains it, "But by the grace of God I am what I am, and his grace toward me was not in vain. On the contrary, I worked harder than any of them, though it was not I, but the grace of God that is with me" (1 Cor. 15:10 ESV). It means that when, by the grace of God we have been chosen to lead and teach, it is our first and foremost obligation to work hard and remember what the Scripture teaches, "that he who began a good work in you will bring it to completion at the day of Jesus Christ" (Philippians 1:16 ESV).

In John 17, Jesus prayed to His father in heaven for His disciples: "do not take them out of this world." As I read His long prayer, I feel that He knew that Christians were free in the judgment of God because of the grace they had been given by the atoning work of Jesus on the cross. Jesus knew that they would be judged by the world, though they are not of the world. The world would consider them out of the norm; for their standards were of God-not of the world. When nonbelievers evaluate those who are believers, their evaluation will be biased; nevertheless, God's standards are not lower than the world's. If you follow the standards of God, you will surpass any worldly standard. However, if the world misinterprets your Godly actions because your actions contradict the world, then you should be thankful and jubilant in the Lord, because for His sake you have been disliked. The Scripture teaches, "For it has been granted to you that for the sake of Christ you should not only believe in him but also suffer for his sake," (Philippians 1:29 ESV).

Step 30 *towards becoming a better leader is to evaluate yourself on a consistent basis.*

Questions and Comments of Day 30

1. If your standards (actions) are in question because they are lower than worldly standards, then you need to evaluate your walk with Christ according to the Scriptures.

Nightly Activity

The Nightly Activity is designed to track the productivity of your everyday life to analyze how the 31 day journey is helping you to become a better person and a better leader. It also serves as a journal. As you advance in your journey, you should look back every day and constantly check the nightly activity page to see whether you are improving. Circle a number you consider to be the overall productivity level of your day. Color the circle you consider to be your spiritual growth level today. See Appendix I.

I observed:_____

_____

I learned:_____

_____

I changed:_____

_____

Review of the day:_____

_____

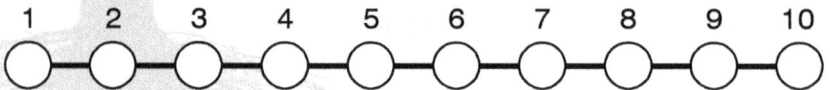

1   2   3   4   5   6   7   8   9   10

WALKING BY FAITH:
Surrender

Romans 7:19-20 is one of the most quoted portions of the Scriptures, referring to our everyday sinful actions, talk, and thoughts. In this portion of Scripture, Paul confesses to the Church of Rome: "For I do not do the good I want, but the evil I do not want is what I keep on doing. Now if I do what I do not want, it is no longer I who do it, but sin that dwells within me." Many times we defend our intentional sinfulness with this verse. But the truth, according to Rom.12, is that we are supposed to be giving our bodies to Christ as a perfect and holy sacrifice, for spiritual worship. Paul writes, "Do not be conformed to this world, but be transformed by the renewal of your mind, that by testing you may discern what is the will of God, what is good and acceptable and perfect" (Rom.12:2 ESV).

Surrender means you trust in the sovereignty of Christ and in Him you have confidence that you will be used for a greater purpose. You give yourself fully and totally to God, keeping nothing behind. Your soul, body and spirit all together become the property of God. When you willingly bring them to the altar of Christ to be presented for a pleasing sacrifice to God, you abide in Him and He abides in you. You are no longer you, but are controlled by the One who resides in you. The apostle John says, "But the anointing that you received from him abides in you, and you have no need that anyone should teach you. But as his anointing teaches you about everything, and is true, and is no lie just as it has taught you, abide in him" (1 John 2:27 ESV).

The moment you give all to God and surrender your will before His will when He abides in you and you abide in Him, a supernatural outside force surrounds you both from within and without. It starts in your heart, that you may be purified from lust, arrogance, quick-temper, and those things which defile your heart and drag you from God and His will. Also the Power (the Holy Spirit) will bring the gifts of the Spirit and leadership into your life. You will be "hospitable, a lover of good, self-controlled, upright, holy, and disciplined" (Tit 1:8 ESV). The work of the Holy Spirit in your heart will be reflected in your bodily actions. And you will (surprisingly) find yourself doing what Paul commanded Titus, "He must hold firm to the trustworthy word as taught, so that he may be able to give instruction in sound doctrine and also to rebuke those who contradict it" (Tit 1:9 ESV).

Although you live in this sinful world, your defense is no longer in your hands, but in God's hand. You will understand the Will of God though your actions, as Paul says, "Accordingly, though I am bold enough in Christ to command you to do what is required, yet for love's sake I prefer to appeal to you—I, Paul, an old man and now a prisoner also for Christ Jesus" (Philemon 1:8-9 ESV). When you surrender yourself to God's will you don't do what your mind asks or society says, but what the mind of God encourages you to do. At times you may feel tempted to speak your mind, but your

Word of Encouragement

"For I know the plans I have for you," declares the LORD, "plans to prosper you and not to harm you, plans to give you hope and a future. Then you will call upon me and come and pray to me, and I will listen to you. You will seek me and find me when you seek me with all your heart." (Jeremiah 29:11-13) surrender will keep you on track to do things through God's will. The will of God is to love; love Him and love each other. 1 Peter 4:19 says, "Therefore let those who suffer according to God's will entrust their souls to a faithful Creator while doing good."

Yesterday a brother who has recently received Christ answered me in a very unexpected way when I asked him, "How are you doing spiritually?" He replied, "Much better than yesterday." I was not expecting a long conversation because I was very busy, but this brother was eager to talk. He told how he had been looking for an answer in the Scriptures, but no one agreed with his interpretation, until he finally found someone on the internet who agreed. His argument was that when we accept Christ we no longer sin; and if we sin, then we have not accepted Christ in our lives. He professed that in the last two months, he had not sinned. I was happy for him; that he was keeping himself pure from whatever he thinks sin is. Then for the next hour and a half I explained how man cannot achieve perfection. That as long as we are in this flesh, our body will always pull us away from God and we will sin: that Jesus is our justification and through him we have access to the throne of God and because of Him we have peace with God the father (Rom. 5:1). If I wanted to win an argument, I could have presented a few verses and probably changed his view, but I wanted him to come to the conclusion on his own. Without Him we are nothing, and surrendering to God's Will is an active part of our faith. We need to fight against our will in order to let God's Will take over in our lives. Jesus said in the garden of Gethsemane, "not My will, but Yours, be done" (Luke 22:42 ESV).

We are not perfect, and never will be in this life; once the sinful flesh is gone, then our temptations are over. Until then, we should strive for perfection and holiness, that we may continually resist temptation. As Jesus said, if we have thought a sinful thought, we have committed a sin. Therefore, if we do fall prey to sin we need to remember that our Savior God is loving and forgiving. Our surrender to the will of God is the only way to walk by faith in Christ.

As a Christian leader, your story has no end. It will continue long after you are gone. It is a never ending story which becomes the trademark of your leadership abilities, and God's unforgettable grace in your life. Your leadership will either make you a legend, or a dark spot on a white garment. People will remember you. Nero, Hitler, and Stalin are a few examples of leaders who thought they were doing well for their nations. Their leadership had a great impact on many; yet today we remember them as horrible stains on history. Whether you are a minor or major leader will be determined by what you are doing today. To write a good story for tomorrow, you need to work on it today. Surrender before God makes you rely on God's wisdom and His pattern. God knows the whole story, even though it is a never-ending one, for He has seen it in eternity. The Psalmist writes, "For you formed my inward parts; you knitted me together in my mother's womb" (Psalm 139:13 ESV). The legacy you will leave behind as a leader will be determined by the strength of your faith in Him.

Recently I came to know a brother who is an international speaker with a ministry among the United Nation's leaders. At first look, this brother may not be one to listen to or to take advice from, but the Holy Spirit (whom he follows) makes him a leader among leaders. You can become a leader of leaders, if you surrender before God.

Today your thirty-one day journey ends, but the never-ending story continues. A new chapter has begun in this story, and the starting line of this chapter is not, "once upon a time there was a king," rather it is, "once upon a time there was an ordinary person with extraordinary leadership skills." It absolutely astonishes the world when ordinary people become extraordinary leaders. Philip was an ordinary man, but left a legacy of a small kingdom to his young son, Alexander, who became Alexander the Great! Mahatma Ghandi was an ordinary person, but history proved him an extraordinary person. Peter, James, John, Mark, Thomas,

Paul and other followers of Christ were ordinary people, but they shook the very foundations of this world so that today, the number of Christians is higher than any other religion. It was not through military invasion that Christianity spread, but through the deep desire to follow Christ-even to the point of death. Walking by faith makes ordinary people extraordinary, because of their belief in the unseen and their confident assurance in Christ makes them extraordinary people. I will close with the following Scriptures:

"Finally, brothers, whatever is true, whatever is honorable, whatever is just, whatever is pure, whatever is lovely, whatever is commendable, if there is any excellence, if there is anything worthy of praise, think about these things" (Philippians 4:8 ESV); "for it is God who works in you, both to will and to work for his good pleasure. Do all things without grumbling or questioning," (Philippians 2:13-14 ESV).

Step 31 towards becoming a better leader is to surrender fully before God's Will.

Questions and Comments of Day 31

1. Have you surrendered your will to God's Will?

2. How do you want people to remember you?

Nightly Activity

The Nightly Activity is designed to track the productivity of your everyday life to analyze how the 31 day journey is helping you to become a better person and a better leader. It also serves as a journal. As you advance in your journey, you should look back every day and constantly check the nightly activity page to see whether you are improving. Circle a number you consider to be the overall productivity level of your day. Color the circle you consider to be your spiritual growth level today. See Appendix I.

I observed:_____

_____

I learned:_____

_____

I changed:_____

_____

Review of the day:_____

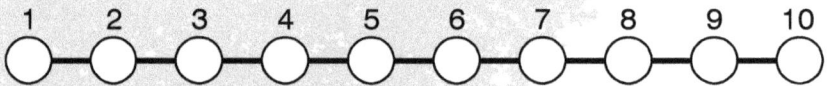

_____

1   2   3   4   5   6   7   8   9   10
○────○────○────○────○────○────○────○────○────○

Nightly Activity—How to calculate your score

Today is your last "Nightly Activity." It is different from the previous nights. You are asked to do a couple of things. First, review **Appendix II (Demo)** and draw a final *Overall Productivity Level (OPL)* and *Spiritual Growth Level (SGL)* Chart to examine the results of your whole months' journey.

Appendix II is simply a demo to help you to understand how it works, while Appendix III is your copy to do the exercise. You are asked to make copies of the "OPL& SGL Chart for the Month" in Appendix IV, to put in your Bible and continue practicing every day (evaluating both overall productivity and spiritual growth).

The 31 day journal will help you to see the result every month, and by the end of the year, you can use the chart from Appendix VI to examine the productivity of the whole year. (The "OPL & SGL Yearly Chart.") The demonstration for the yearly chart is available in Appendix V. It is essential to see (with your eyes every day) where you are heading. If you need a change in your leadership style, in everyday life, or in ministry in order to be more productive for the Kingdom of God, it will be seen. This process will hold you accountable before God, and help you to continually move forward.

Review of the 31 day daily exercise

You are asked to calculate the total points of all 31 days to see what you have obtained (out of the total 300 points). Do it for both the *"Overall Productivity Level"* charts and the *"Spiritual Growth Level"* charts to see the comparison of both lines. Please follow the Appendix II model. You can also break up the time periods according to your own calendar.

APPENDIX I

Overall Productivity Level Line

This is my prayer: that this test may help you to see, physically, where you are heading in terms of your leadership and ministry. Many times as servants of God we feel lost, burned out, exhausted, unsatisfied, and even angry, because we expend our all but there are no results. It makes us question whether we are making any difference. If our leadership is effective, then, skills are developing. In other situations, we are very confident and do not want to change our methods to enhance the kingdom of God. I pray, as you progress through the 31-day journey, that you may observe your life and ministry very closely. For instance, what are the things in your ministry and leadership style contributing to your overall productivity? (60%, 80%, 20%, 10%, or even none, in the total productivity of your ministry and life?) Also, what are the lessons you are learning every day and on the basis of those learned lessons, what changes are you willing to make?

If I count the productivity of my whole day, considering what went well and what went wrong, after analyzing I may come to the conclusion that my overall productivity was average. Considering 1=poor and 10=extraordinary I may choose 4. Thus, I will circle 4.

Spiritual Growth Level Line

When you are serving in a ministry, it becomes very challenging to separate your personal spiritual growth from the spiritual growth of your ministry. Your relationship with God should be the top priority, and you should not be deluded by the productivity or growth of your ministry. Therefore, the following line will help you every day to evaluate your personal spiritual growth separately from your overall growth and productivity. On the SGL line you would not include anything other than your personal relationship with God. This is a visual evaluation of your walk with God. Considering 1=poor and 10=extraordinary, I may choose 4. Thus, I will fill the 4th circle.

Overall Productivity Level Line (OPC)

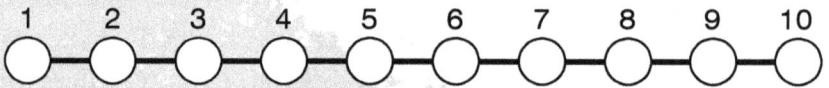

1   2   3   4   5   6   7   8   9   10

Spiritual Growth Level Line (SGL)

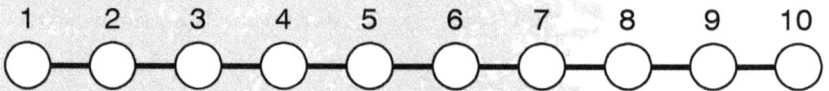

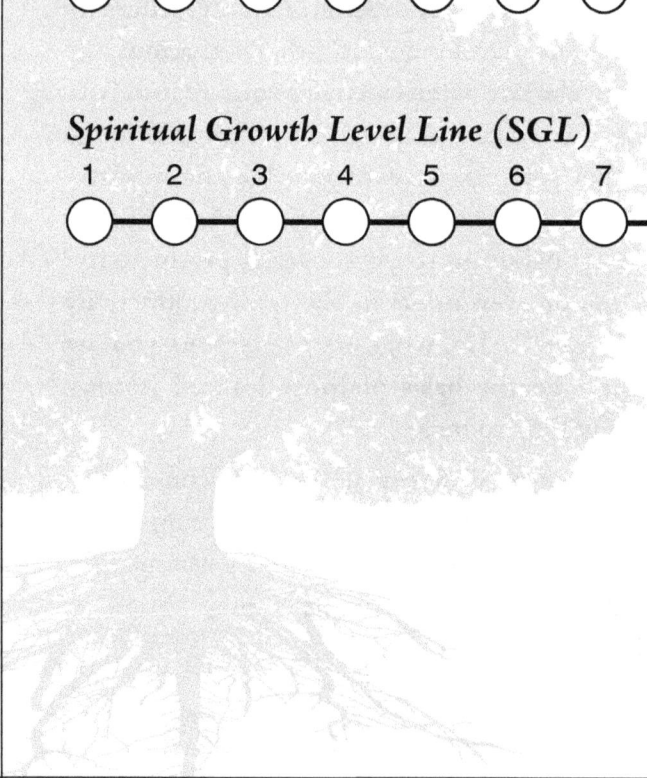

1   2   3   4   5   6   7   8   9   10

APPENDIX II

Demo of Overall Productivity Level &
Spiritual Growth Level Chart for 31 Days

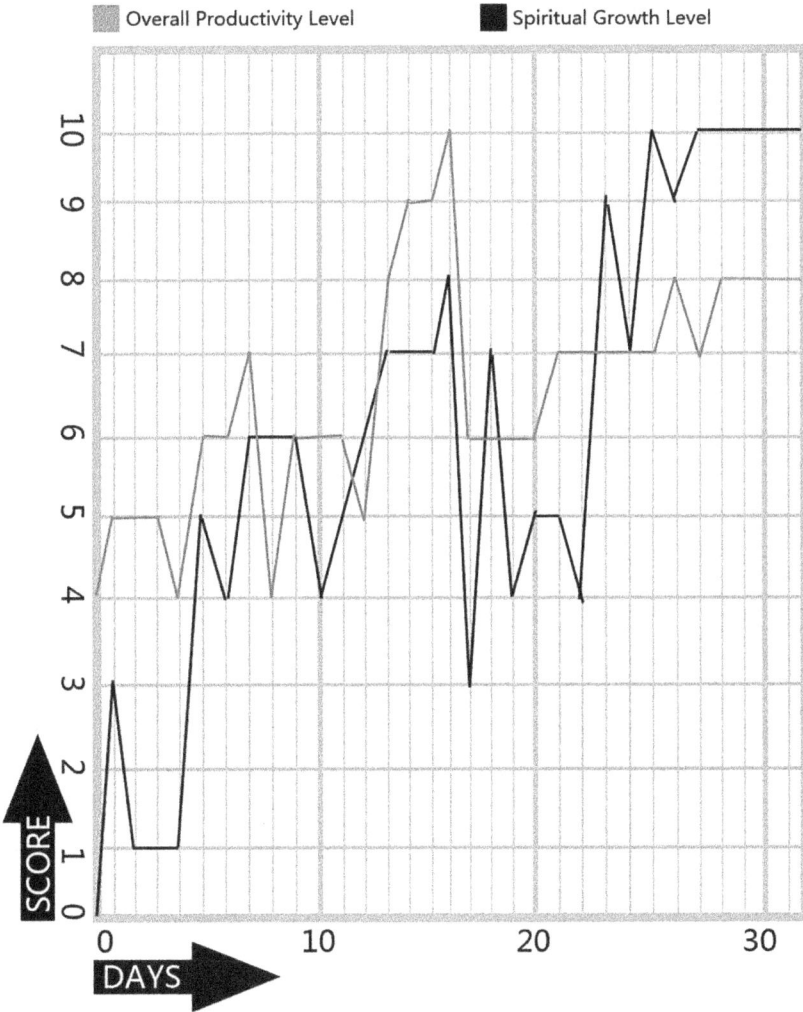

Overall Productivity Level   Spiritual Growth Level

SCORE

DAYS

APPENDIX III

Chart Your Overall Productivity Level &
Spiritual Growth Level Chart for 31 Days

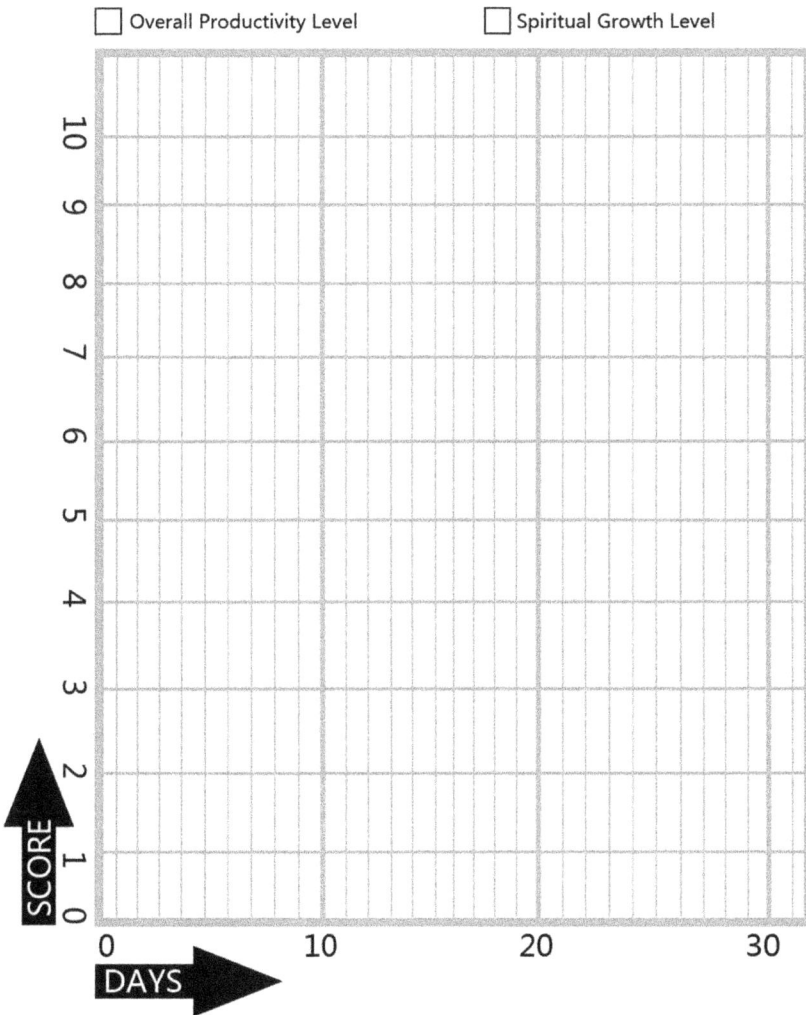

☐ Overall Productivity Level   ☐ Spiritual Growth Level

SCORE ↑

10
9
8
7
6
5
4
3
2
1
0

0   10   20   30

DAYS →

APPENDIX IV

Your Overall Productivity Level & Spiritual Growth Level Chart for 31 Days—Keep This in Your Bible

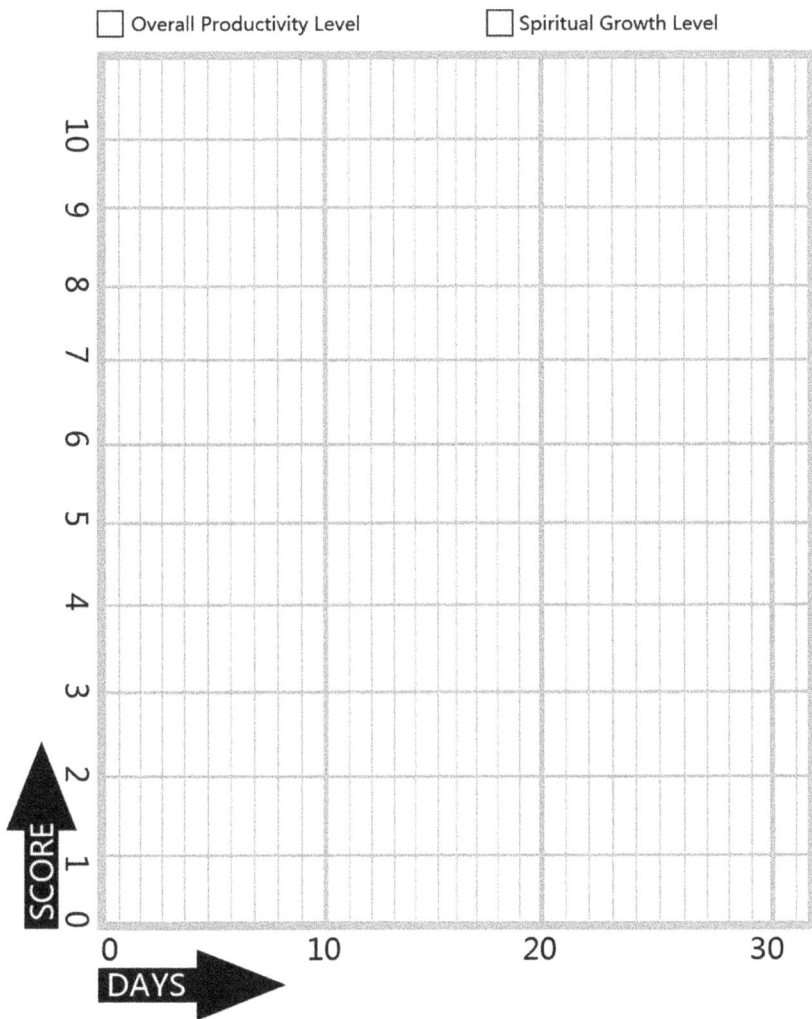

☐ Overall Productivity Level   ☐ Spiritual Growth Level

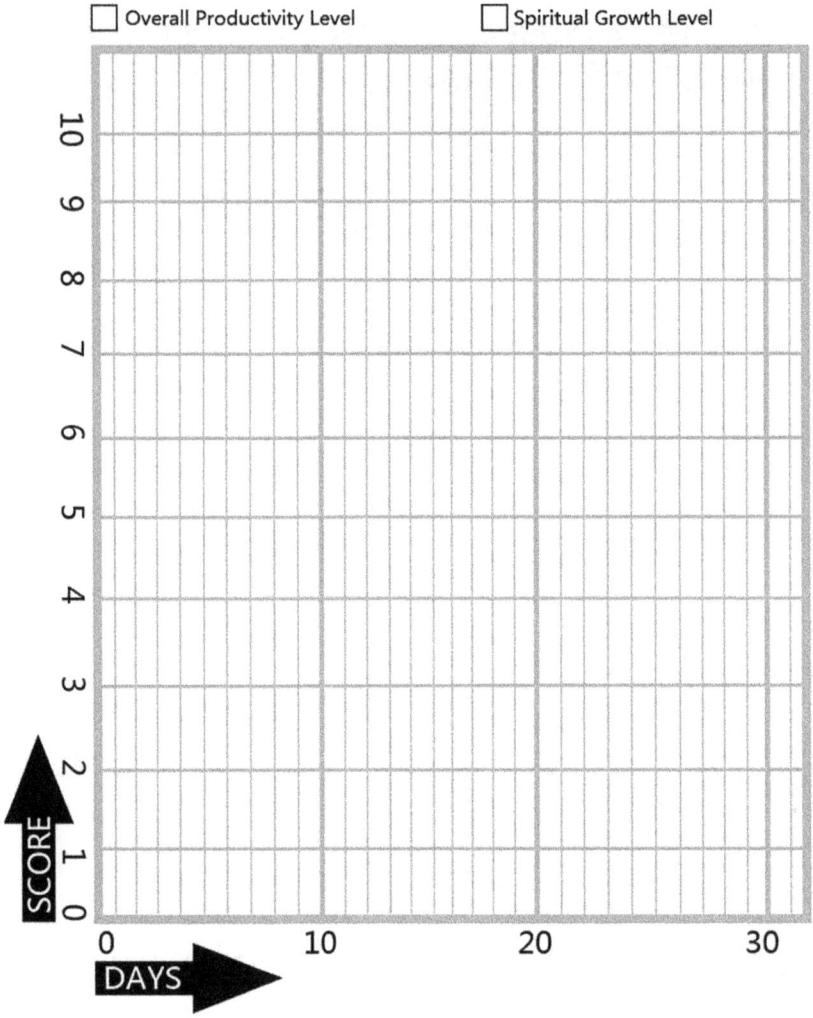

☐ Overall Productivity Level ☐ Spiritual Growth Level

SCORE

DAYS

APPENDIX V

Demo of Overall Productivity Level &
Spiritual Growth Level Yearly Chart

Now here is your chance to see the progress and productivity of a whole year in one glance. You can use any color to differentiate your "Overall Productivity Level" from Spiritual Growth Level. Also rather than months, you can use the starting date and ending date of either 30/31days evaluation.

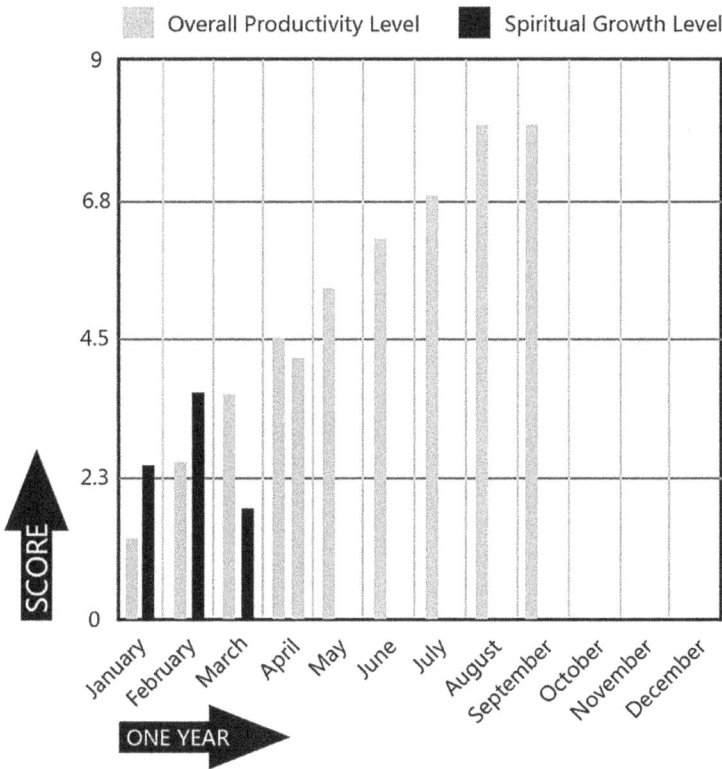

APPENDIX VI

Your Overall Productivity Level &
Spiritual Growth Level Yearly Chart

A fter counting, the total points you have obtain in OPL and SGL for each 31 days evaluation or 30 days, draw vertical line just as in the example you see in Appendix V. Please choose two different colors to show OPL and SGL lines.

Considering each thin line a sample of 100, the following vertical line starting with "0" goes up to "300." Thus, you will draw a line vertically within the frame of the month to show how many points you have obtained each month.

Use the blank chart on the following page.

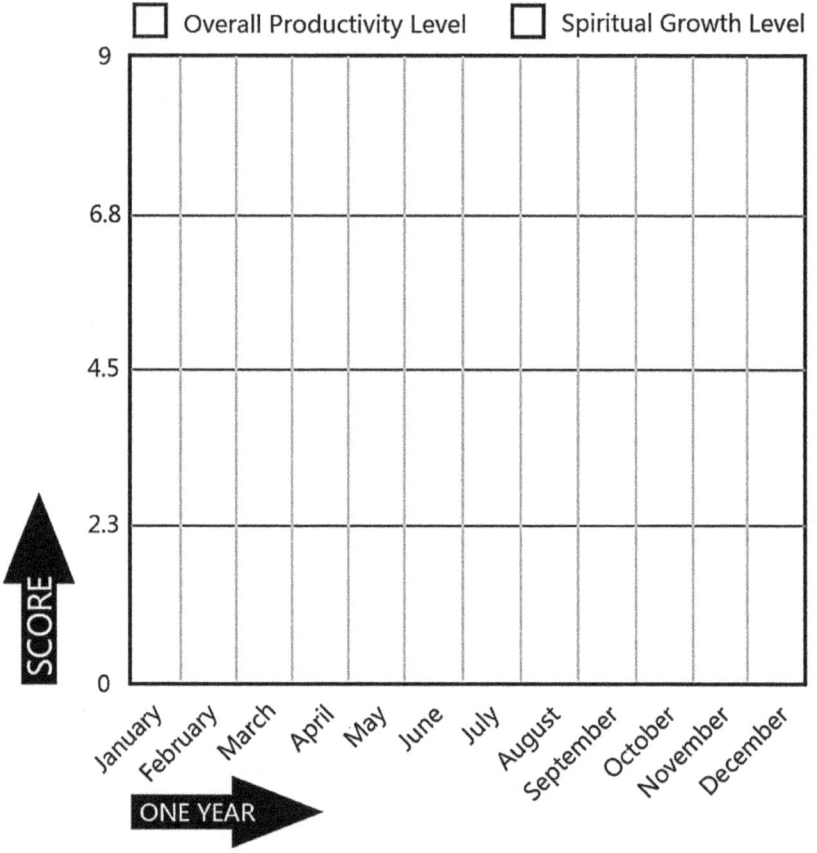

□ Overall Productivity Level   □ Spiritual Growth Level

SCORE

9

6.8

4.5

2.3

0

January February March April May June July August September October November December

ONE YEAR

APPENDIX VII

Brooklyn Bridge, NYC, NY, USA

BIBLIOGRAPHY

Australian Centre for Leadership for Women. "Food for Thought: Memorable Quotes." Quote by Dr. Ann Marie E. McSwain. Accessed May 14, 2012. http://www.leadershipforwomen.com.au/quotes.htm.

Barna, George. *Think like Jesus: Make the Right Decision Every Time*. Brentwood, TN: Integrity Publishers, 2003.

Budziszewski, J. "Natural Law Revealed," *First Things* (2008) Accessed May 11, 2012. http://www.firstthings.com/article/2008/11/003-natural-law-revealed-34.

Byrne, Gabriel J. and Bradley, Frank. "Culture's influence on leadership efficiency: How personal and national cultures affect leadership style."*Journal of Business Research*, Volume 60, Issue 2, (February 2007) 168-175.

Carlisle, Howard M. *Management: Concepts, Methods and Applications,* 2nd ed. Chicago: Science Research Associates, 1982. 211.

Cosgrove, Mark P. *Foundations of Christian Thought: Faith, Learning, and the Christian Worldview.* Grand Rapids, MI: Kregel Publications, 2006.

Dictionary.com. "Vision." Accessed May 16, 2012, http://dictionary.reference.com/browse/vision.

Drucker, Peter F. *The Effective Executive: The Definitive Guide to Getting the Right Things Done.* New York: HarperBusiness Essentials, 1966.

Inspirational Quotes. "Leadership Quotations." Harold R. McAlindon. Accessed on May 9, 2012. http://www.inspirational-quotes.info/leadership.html

Inspiring short stories. Accessed June 16, 2010, http://www. indianchild. com/inspiring_stories.htm

Kouzes, Jim & Posner, Barry. *The Leadership Challenge: How To Get Extraordinary Things Done In Organizations.* San Francisco, California: Jossey-Bass Inc, Publishers, 1987.

Malphurs, Aubrey. *Maximizing Your Effectiveness: How to Discover and Develop Your Divine Design.* Grand Rapids, MI: Baker Publishing Group, 2006.

Maxwell, John C. *Developing the Leader Within You.* Nashville, TN: Thomas Nelson, 1993.

Page, Nanette & Cheryl E. Czuba. "Empowerment: What Is It?" Journal of Extension, 1999. Accessed January 26, 2010, http://www.joe.org/joe/1999october/comm1.php.

Robbins, Harvey and Michael Finley. Why Change Doesn't Work: Why Initiatives Go Wrong and How to Try Again – And Succeed. London: Orion Publishing Company, 1997.

Stembridge, Allen F. "Teacher Motivation: An Essential Requirement in the Integration of Faith and Learning in Seventh-Day Adventist Colleges." Institute for Christian Teaching website, 1989. Accessed October 11, 2007, http://www.aiias.edu/ict/vol_04/04cc_169-189.htm.

Tucker, Ruth A. From Jerusalem to Irian Jaya: A Biographical History of Christian Missions. Grand Rapids, MI: Zondervan, 1983.

World Bank. *A Guide to the World Bank, Second Edition.* Washington, DC: The International Bank for Reconstruction and Development/ The World Bank, 2007.

References

Bauer, Susan Wise. "A Neutral Education." The Well-Trained Mind: Classical Education for the Next Generation, 2009. Accessed January 26, 2010, http://www.welltrainedmind.com/a-neutral-education/.

Gaebelein, Frank E. *The Pattern of God's Truths*. Chicago, Illinois: Moody Press, 1980.

Schaeffer, Francis A. *How Then Should We Live?* Chicago, IL: Crossway Books, 1996.

Sire, James W. *The Universe Next Door: A Basic Worldview Catalog* (4th ed.) Downers Grove, IL: InterVarsity Press, 2004.

Stader, David L. *Law and Ethics in Educational Leadership.* Upper Saddle River, NJ: Pearson Education, Inc, 2007.

Spunky Homeschool. (2005). Education is Not Neutral. Retrieved January 26, 2010, http://spunkyhomeschool.blogspot.com/2005/09/education-is-not-neutral.html

"Is World View Neutral Education Possible and Desirable?" by SigneSandsmark http://www.eureca-online.org/en/reviews/index.html Review by Clarence Joldersma references: http://www.thefreedictionary.com/Weltanschauung

Unknown. (2009). The Laws of Nature and Nature's God. Retrieved from http://www.lonang.com/

ABOUT THE MINISTRY OF ANM

ANM Publications is a ministry initiative of Advancing Native Missions

Advancing Native Missions (ANM) is a U.S.-based Christian missions agency. However, unlike many such agencies which are involved in sending missionaries from America to other places around the world, ANM works with indigenous missionaries. Indigenous (or native) missionaries are Christian workers who minister within their own sphere of influence proclaiming the Gospel of Jesus Christ to their own people. ANM then works to connect Christians in America with these brothers and sisters, to equip and encourage them. Our goal is to build relationships of love and trust between indigenous missionaries and North American individuals and churches. In this way, the entire body of Christ becomes involved in completing the Great Commission. **"And this gospel of the kingdom shall be preached in all the world as a witness to all nations, and then the end shall come"** (Matthew 24:14).

If you would like to know how you can become an effective coworker with native missionaries to reach the unreached for Jesus Christ, contact ANM at requests@adnamis.org, call us at 540-456-7111, or visit our website: www.advancingnativemissions.com.

www.ingramcontent.com/pod-product-compliance
Lightning Source LLC
LaVergne TN
LVHW011223080426
835509LV00005B/290